"Lilit Marcus has written perhaps the only book so fun it can actually double as a beach read. Chock full of pop culture references and caricatures that will make you laugh out loud, *Save the Assistants* also gets down to business with its no-nonsense advice for making the best of your entry-level tenure. Marcus' popular online community—and now her book of the same name—has transformed being an assistant into an exclusive rite of passage."
—ALEXANDRA LEVIT,
author of *They Don't Teach Corporate in College*
and *New Job, New You*

"Lilit brings the same charm, sharp wit, and knowledge to the *Save the Assistants* book that she does to her always-engaging blog. It's a must-read for all assistants, and truly anyone in the modern workplace could benefit from the advice and anecdotes she shares about surviving life in a cubicle."
—KAREN GOLDSTEIN,
blogger/writer of Advice from a PA, and former
personal assistant to many well-known faces in Hollywood

"Funny and practical, *Save the Assistants* is not only the New Testament for assistants but the Bible for bosses. Thanks to Lilit Marcus, there will be better hiring and less firing!"
—ELLEN GORDON REEVES,
author of *Can I Wear My Nose Ring to the Interview?*

"*Save the Assistants* is a must-have resource for those toiling under the weight of the ground floor. Lilit Marcus, who has spent years shining a bright light on the dark-humor side of assistant life (all while on the clock as an assistant), may not save you from fetching a cup of coffee for your boss, but she will show you how to salvage your wage-slave existence and make a quick leap to a higher rung inside the workplace morass."
—JEFFREY YAMAGUCHI,
author of *Working for the Man*

"Lilit Marcus has moxie. This book offers heaps of practical advice for facing down the triple-headed demon of pressing financial need, high expectations for yourself, and a job that doesn't seem to let you meet them. *Save the Assistants* is nothing less than a public service."

—MEGAN HUSTAD,
author of *How to Be Useful*

"Lilit Marcus's advice to assistants on how to handle a multitude of evil and morally bereft bosses is brilliant, pragmatic, and fun. If you are an assistant, this book will help you escape from the indentured servitude of your first real job sooner so that you can move on to your dream career. If you are a boss, this book will help you develop empathy so that you can avoid becoming one of its subjects! A must-read for anyone who had visions of making it big on nothing but a shoestring and a college degree, but somehow ended up at a tedious desk job instead."

—VICKY OLIVER,
author of *301 Smart Answers to Tough Interview Questions*
and *301 Smart Answers to Tough Business Etiquette Questions*

Save the Assistants

Save the Assistants

A Guide to Surviving and Thriving
in the Workplace

Lilit Marcus

Illustrations by
Ben Schwartz

HYPERION
NEW YORK

Copyright © 2010 Lilit Marcus

Illustrations by Ben Schwartz

All rights reserved. No part of this book may be used or reproduced in any manner whatsoever without the written permission of the Publisher. Printed in the United States of America. For information address Hyperion, 114 Fifth Avenue, New York, New York, 10011.

Library of Congress Cataloging-in-Publication Data has been applied for.

ISBN 978-1-4013-1017-2

Hyperion books are available for special promotions and premiums. For details contact the HarperCollins Special Markets Department in the New York office at 212-207-7528, fax 212-207-7222, or e-mail spsales@harpercollins.com.

FIRST EDITION

10 9 8 7 6 5 4 3 2 1

Acknowledgments

It takes a village to save an assistant. And without Ashley Seashore, who was my friend first and my collaborator later, I never would have survived at my first assistant job. If not for Ashley, *Save the Assistants* would have just been a thing I thought about for a while and never followed through on. The Web site also wouldn't exist without Justin Ouellette's excellent photography or without Michael Lange, who built the mainframe and provided countless hours of free tech support.

Beyond the blog, this book owes a great debt to the guidance and support of my agent, Rebecca Gradinger of Fletcher and Company, and my editor, Nina Shield, as well as the rest of the wonderful team at Hyperion. Also, this book truly came to life thanks to Ben Schwartz's brilliant caricatures in the Bossary.

Some other people also deserve thanks here for reasons too manifold to list: my parents, Joel and Harriet Marcus; DJ Waletzky; Stefanie Lieberman; Paul Lucas; Matthew Caldecutt; Erik Trinidad; Kimba Knight-Hart; and Lily Kosner.

Contents

Introduction

Let's be totally honest: I started a Web site called Save the Assistants because I hated my job. I wish I could tell you that I quit said job right after the first in-the-bathroom cryfest and immediately became a spunky *Norma Rae*–type heroine, but the truth is that it took some time to build up enough courage to walk out. I may have been desperate, but I wasn't stupid—living in New York was not free, and I needed even the meager $28K salary.

I grew up in North Carolina and attended a state university there. A couple of months after graduating, armed with a degree in English Lit and dreams of "making it" as a writer (whatever that means), I moved to New York City. I didn't have any friends or connections in the city, so like a lot of other young people, I applied for every job that was even loosely related to what I wanted to do. In other words, I spent a lot of time temping. One day, the woman who ran my temp agency got me an interview to be the receptionist at a big media company. Although being a receptionist wasn't my dream job, the company sounded interesting and I figured that while I was sitting at the front desk I would also have time to keep sending out résumés and obsessively refreshing the Craigslist job boards. The company, which we'll just call the Evil Empire, hired me right away. Then, on my first day, while I was unpacking my stuff at the reception desk, the office manager casually informed me that I was also going to be someone's assistant. Surprise!

Being an assistant at the Evil Empire meant you spent lots of time getting screamed at for stuff like stapling something in a way your boss didn't like. Although most of our bosses at the Evil Empire were backstabby and competitive with one other, the assistants didn't follow suit and became a pretty close-knit group. One of the assistants I bonded with was named Ashley Seashore. Unlike me, who'd had only internships, Ashley had a decent amount of work experience, and she helped me figure out the everyday ins and outs of working in an office. She taught me about all the things I hadn't learned in college but desperately needed to know at a job—like when to BCC people on e-mails, how to handle criticism, and what to say when you got blamed for something that wasn't your fault. If not for her, I would have either been fired or had a nervous breakdown by the end of the second week.

We assistants got along pretty well and formed an unofficial support group for one another. Somebody always checked on you when you had a hangover, helped salvage the PowerPoint presentation you'd totally ruined, covered your phone when you had to sneak out for a smoke break, and took you out for lunch on your birthday. At some point, while chatting on the internal messaging system (any IM program was blocked from office computers, as were Hotmail, Yahoo, Gmail, eBay, and—eventually—a little site called Save the Assistants), Ashley and I decided it would be really cool if there was some kind of online network for assistants, a virtual version of the happy hours we had with our assistant crew. And when one didn't exist, we decided to make one. After we both finally bailed from the Evil Empire, had time to detox, and moved on to better jobs that actually provided us with dignity, Save the Assistants (STA) was born.

At first, it seemed like the only people reading STA were us and our friends, and some of them sent in horror stories that we published under fake names (a note: unless an assistant specifically says it's okay to use his or her real name, all horror stories on STA—and in this book—are assigned pseudonyms). But, before we knew it, our traffic started to grow. We got linked to popular blogs and mentioned in magazine and newspaper articles. It seemed that being a mistreated, beleaguered assistant was a pretty common phenomenon. Even people who were no longer assistants and had been in better jobs for years still smarted from the way they were treated back when they were getting started. It turned out that our little "virtual happy hour" was a pretty crowded bar. In addition to horror stories, we started running items about celebrity assistants, updates about workplace laws and other policies that affected entry-level workers, reviews of career advice books, articles about assistant-centric TV shows and movies like *The Devil Wears Prada* and *Ugly Betty*, and more. Mail came from as far away as London and Sydney. If there's anything I've learned, it's that having a shitty job is a pretty universal experience.

The most rewarding part of running the site was striking up friendships with assistants from all over the world. I developed offline relationships with some of the site's regular contributors and counseled them on how to handle their bosses. Sometimes readers would e-mail me to let me know that they'd quit their jobs and, even though I may have lost them as readers now that they're not assistants, it's pretty sweet to know that some of the things posted on my site have helped people kick butt in their careers. One of the assistants who wound up finding her dream job was Ashley—although the new hours and responsibilities meant that she didn't have time for STA anymore, I was more than happy to take it over. Luckily, she still e-mails me the occasional link to a story that would fit in well on the site.

So that's where this book comes in. Why just cry about your mistreatment over drinks with friends when you can sing it to the world? And if you're worried about protecting that boss of yours, just remember one thing: if they didn't want you to talk about it, they shouldn't have behaved that way.

However, this book is about more than horror stories. Yeah, I've got a lot of those. But I also have some really awesome stories about assistants who made it out and up and are now proudly well-behaved bosses with their very own assistants. I've gotten to know a lot about the virtues of workplace distractions. I've even managed to come up with some of my own theories about how to identify certain boss personalities and also, most important, how to spot a fellow assistant who is suffering from the much-dreaded Stockholm syndrome.

In many industries, being an assistant is still the only way in. You have to learn the ropes before you can move up, so your career is essentially in the hands of your boss. This isn't always a terrible thing, because there are decent and great bosses out there. But, sadly, many assistants still have to deal with Past Their Primes, Overstressers, Functional Illiterates, Martyrs, and Frenemies. I am here to help, so read on.

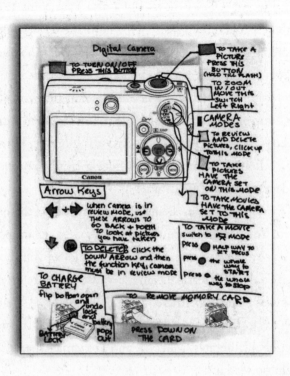

A Millennial Assistant Manifesto

The relationship between bosses and assistants is kind of like the one between parents and children: the latter thinks the former is boring, uptight, and uncool; the former finds the latter lazy, selfish, and entitled. They're both a little bit right and a little bit wrong.

Why is it that the generation currently entering the workforce—Generation Y, or "Millennials," for lack of better terms—has earned a reputation of being spoiled brats who don't want to work? It's certainly not unusual for the "established" group to hate the newcomers. Our grandparents thought our parents were a bunch of slackers. That's the way offices work: the veterans think they know the best way to do things and don't appreciate a bunch of new hires telling them to change or do things differently. The most obvious place that the divide between generations becomes apparent is technology. As technology changes ever more rapidly, it's the younger generation—aka, the most recent hires—that usually has the best grasp on how to quickly and efficiently use computers, e-mail, iPhones, and the rest. For an older worker, imagine not only trying to keep up with the constantly updating technology in the office, but the frustration of seeing someone younger and less experienced than you figuring it all out with absolutely no problem.

I find that what gets read as the "entitlement" of Gen-Yers in the workplace is usually the result of one of two things: the assistant's genuine feeling of having been baited and switched from the interview process to the actual reality of the position granted, or, in less frequent cases, assistants who actually feel a sense of entitlement— those few who give the rest of us a bad name.

While it's an incredibly small minority, there are indeed twenty-somethings out there with trust funds, well-connected parents, and tremendous egos who show up for their first day on the job utterly horrified that they're expected to do actual work instead of be rewarded simply for existing. Pete Campbell on the first season of the show *Mad Men* is a classic example of this type. He's from a wealthy society family, went to the best and most exclusive schools, and resents the fact that his bosses at the Madison Avenue advertising agency Sterling Cooper expect him to do his job. His name and pedigree allow him to leverage his family connections and advance in his field, but he's not terribly good at his job. All the while, he's petulant, conceited, and treats fellow employees—both his subordinates and his equals—like dirt. However, the percentage of Pete Campbells in your average pool of fresh-from-college workers is pretty tiny. Most of these kids have enough good connections that they don't even have to bother with the pretense of an entry-level job in the first place. While they're out there, it's sad that such a meager fraction of Gen-Yers give the rest of the bunch a bad name. The thing is, these people exist in every generation. They're by no means a new invention. And yet, every year a new crop of workers is forced to do everything they can to not be perceived as a Pete Campbell, all the while envying him. After all, if *we* had his trust fund, *we'd* be starting a nonprofit organization to feed starving orphans in Africa, not sitting around the office and whining.

The other employees who get branded with the E-word are the baited and switched. The majority of "entitled" employees come from this pool. I should know, as I was one of them.

In her follow-up to the best-selling book *Nickel and Dimed*, in which she spent a year trying to live on a typical minimum-wage salary and weighed in on the plight of America's working poor, Barbara Ehrenreich wrote *Bait and Switch: The (Futile) Pursuit of the American Dream*. The 2005 book followed Ehrenreich as she went "undercover" as a woman reentering the hiring pool after some time off. She detailed experiences with companies who "sold" an employee on one job, only to completely change the job description as soon as the candidate started working. This happened to me: the Evil Empire knowingly kept me in the dark about the actual nature of my job while I was interviewing for it. During the interview, the

HR manager asked me lots of detailed, probing questions about my ambitions, my dreams, and where I could see myself in five years. I'd had a couple of interviews for administrative jobs before, but never one where they were so curious to know about what I wanted out of my career. She also paid close attention to my résumé and asked lots of questions about what I'd studied in college and how I felt about New York so far. I came out of the interview full of hope and excitement.

Knowing that no one would want to accept a full-time assistant/full-time receptionist job that essentially required you to be in two places at once, all day long, thus setting yourself up for total failure, the company remained as vague as they could with my job description until I came in to start working. I often think it's a miracle anyone ever does well at an assistant job, even when they knew exactly what they were getting into. Ehrenreich would probably agree—she witnessed so many cases of burnout, despair, and anxiety among workers (not just entry-level ones) who'd come in expecting one thing and wound up living another that she was surprised anyone manages to hold a job, ever.

The detractors of Generation Y do have one thing pretty much right—we *were* indulged, mostly by parents who believed that their children were special, perfect, and better than everyone else's children. While it's certainly no crime to love your kids and think they're the greatest, not every parent did the best job simultaneously imbuing their children with a sense of reality. Like many other kids, particularly white middle-class kids, I grew up being told that when I was an adult I could do anything I wanted if I just tried hard enough. By the time I went to my public state university, professors and career counselors told me that simply having a college degree meant that I was guaranteed a real, rewarding career as soon as I graduated. The notion that a college degree equals lifelong success is one that was built in the 1940s and '50s, when a small percentage of the population went to a university. It was true then. It isn't true now that so many more Americans not only go to college but get graduate degrees, but people keep on saying it—and, consciously or unconsciously, believing it. I sure did. On graduation day, my parents grinned and took photographs of me in my cap and gown. And then I went out in search of my first job.

As I sent out résumés and rewrote cover letters, I realized the dizzying whir of "IneedajobIneedajobIneedajob" was spinning around so quickly that I didn't have any time to dissect exactly what "I need a job" meant. Yes, I had to be practical—I was a real live grown-up now and was responsible for paying rent and buying groceries. But I'd been on a sort of conveyer belt my whole life—go to high school, go to college, get a job—and I had never stopped to wonder if the "normal" path was one I actually wanted to take, or one I was following because I thought I was supposed to. Many college graduates like myself, especially ones with pressing financial needs, get so caught up in this headspace that they don't have time or energy to really think critically about what sort of job they might like. I prepared for my first day at work like I'd gotten ready for the first day of school—I picked out a cute outfit, set my alarm clock, and couldn't sleep because I was so consumed with thoughts about what the people in the office were going to be like and if they'd be nice to me. I was a little girl playing dress-up, imagining myself a character in a movie about working. I was no more prepared to have an office job than I was to fly an airplane.

Obviously, once I got that first job—at one point I remember telling Ashley my business card should read "Professional Whipping Girl"—reality came crashing down around me pretty quickly. The first day I spent doing nothing except answering phone calls, taking messages, and bringing coffee. I was indignant: I went through four years of college for *this*? I got huffy when I was passed over for interesting, relevant-to-my-skills work in favor of typing, taking dictation, and other stuff that made me feel like a relic from the 1950s, which didn't help when my boss insisted on referring to me as his secretary. Once, when he was screaming at me about yet another thing I'd done wrong, the dreaded word— "entitled"—escaped from his trollish mouth: "You are so entitled."

And that was when it hit me, or when it began to hit

me. What comes off looking like entitlement (a lot of "You know, I graduated summa cum laude, do you think maybe next time I can *write* the press release instead of just fax it to people?") is the aftereffect of being baited and switched. Not only had my employers misled me, but so had guidance counselors, career coaches, teachers, the media, and even my parents. Although all of them (except the employers) had had only the best of intentions when they told me I was destined for greatness, they'd unwittingly set me up for a pretty colossal failure. While it was obviously not realistic of me to expect to waltz into a magazine office and immediately be offered a cushy staff writing position, I didn't think I'd spend the first few years of my career working as an office drone, desperately trying to snare even a tiny byline way in the back of the magazine. Something didn't fit. And that something was that I had absolutely no idea what it meant to be an assistant or, more simply, what it meant to have a job. I missed the intellectual thrill of college. One of my coworkers said she felt like she "turned her brain off" when she came into work every day. I felt an incredible disconnect, and, furthermore, I felt that I'd regressed.

My boss felt a sense of entitlement from me, and I can't blame him for that. He had no way of knowing how totally invalidated I felt by my job, because there was no way I ever would have told him. I thought of myself as a tortured intellectual whose talents were being cruelly thwarted. All my boss cared about was whether I did my job—and, to be perfectly honest, a lot of the time I didn't. My boss and I existed in two separate worlds. And, as a result, we were a horrible fit for each other. Our incompatibility made it a war to get even the most basic tasks accomplished. It wasn't just bad for us, it was bad for the company.

The question is, how do we live both truths at the same time? How do we simultaneously believe that the workplace is cold and unforgiving and that we are awesome and deserve better? The most important thing to remember is that there is a huge difference between having a job and having a career. Just because you spend your first year in the workforce doing nothing but organizing the conference room and color-coding folders doesn't mean that you're doomed to spend your entire life doing nothing else. There's a reason the phrase "paying your dues" exists: it's because getting to the top of any profession involves a whole lot of hard work. What you'll learn to do in this book is pay your dues in a smart way.

First, you must remember that there's nothing inherently wrong with being an assistant. Almost everyone has to start low on the totem pole of the industry they want to work in. But if your ambition is to be something other than an assistant, you have to learn to put the job in perspective. In the short term, you can choose to be on autopilot during the day but pursue your outside interests on your own time. If you're still clinging to the memories of your college glory days, remember which things about college made you really happy, and find a way to keep them a part of your life. Many of the happiest assistants I've met also played bass in a band, acted in an improv troupe, coached a team in an intramural basketball league, or volunteered at an animal shelter. If you hate your job and don't want it to define you, you should be involved in other activities that fulfill you in different ways so that there are lots of other things that *can* define you.

In the long term, you need to do your job—and do it really, really well. Don't just make coffee—make the best damn coffee anybody in the office has ever tasted. Because what better way to show off your skills than by kicking ass at every single project you're assigned, no matter its size? If you want your assistant job to be a stepping stone to something greater, you need to realize that you're not going to get promoted by sitting around, complaining about how much you hate your life, and sucking at your job. The only thing that'll get you is fired or—even worse—trapped in perpetual assistant limbo, growing angrier and more disgruntled every day. So pay your dues, but pay them intelligently—network with people at your company, constantly redo your résumé to reflect new skills you've learned on the job, learn every single thing you can about how your industry works, and take on extra work to prove your dedication. It might help to get through a particularly bad day at the office by remembering how fortunate you are just to have a job in the first place, especially if you had a long and unsatisfying job search process that left you so broke you ate Ramen and PB&Js every day. By landing a gig, you've already accomplished something. That shouldn't stop you from looking for better work, using the office copier to print out extra copies of your résumé, and sneaking out during your lunch break to go on an interview, but it should help to ground you on those days when you're tempted to just storm out of the office and never look back.

There's no law saying you can't simultaneously hate your job and also want to do well at it: in fact, it's a lot easier to be ambitious when you have work that backs up your ambition. So clean your desk, grab a cup of coffee (make that two—one for the boss and one for you), and do your part to help erase the E-word forever.

Save the Assistants

ONE

The Daily Life of an Assistant

I thought I could see the light at the end
of the tunnel, but it was just some bastard with
a torch, bringing me more work.

—DAVID BRENT
(Ricky Gervais) on *The Office* (U.K.)

It all starts with a desk. It may not be a very big or a very sturdy desk—in fact, it's probably part of a cubicle. But it's yours. Soon, you will learn—maybe the first time you've had to stifle tears in the bathroom stall when you hear someone else come in, or when your boss follows you halfway down the hall so she can keep yelling at you—that your desk is the only thing in the office that truly belongs to you, the only place where you have even a modicum of safety.

Desks are familiar. After all, remember college? You were so good at college: sleeping until eleven instead of noon meant that you were a go-getter, writing essays about your difficult adolescence was considered a valuable skill, and no one cared when you worked on your term paper as long as you finished it on time. Now that you're done with college, it's time to get a job. That is the natural progression of things, right? I mean, that's what everybody else does—and those college loans certainly won't pay themselves off.

So now you've gotten yourself a job. Turns out that no one in the interview cared what your GPA was or how you started an extracurricular brownie-baking club on campus. So much for being an all-star athlete or the president of your sorority. Suddenly, the only skills that anybody cares about are whether you can make a good cup of coffee and keep four calls on hold at the same time. What gives?

At first, when you get offered that elusive job, you're all "Yay, they hired *me*, they picked *me*!" and you dork out, buying new pens and trying to figure out if that black blazer makes you look smart and professional or uptight and boring. After all, you had to send out hundreds of résumés and cover letters just to get a handful of interviews, and *finally* one panned out into gainful employment. All you can think about is the money you're going to make and what you're going to do with it— you'll pay off your credit card debt or finally end the deferment on your student loans . . . or maybe you'll get those shoes you've been coveting or the Wii you were planning to ask your parents for as a Christmas present. You're on top of the world, and what could possibly knock you off your perch? I'll tell you: actually working.

Pretty soon you'll realize that there's a difference between how jobs are portrayed in the media or by your career counselor and how most of them actually are. It's normal to be depressed, dejected, or in some way unhappy when you start a job—especially if it's your first one. Have you ever noticed how on the TV show *The Office* (at least the U.S. version), even though they're at work all the time, most of the story lines are about them interacting with one another and not really about them doing any work? It is boring to watch people make PowerPoint presentations on their computers or file stuff for five hours, and no TV show is ever going to rely on that for drama. It turns out that it's fun to watch Dwight Schrute on television, but it is really annoying to work with him in real life.

You may also think a job is a lot like an internship. I've actually found that internships are often way better than jobs. You may not be getting paid, but because you're not getting paid you don't have the same pressure, deadlines, and fear of getting fired that a salaried employee has. While lots of internships are useful for teaching you about an industry or even giving you a sense of how a typical office works, coming in for four hours a week and working with only a few select employees doesn't paint an accurate picture of what a real nine-to-five job is like. Most interns, because they're unpaid and/or temporary employees, are kept away from major meetings, finances, and anything with too much responsibility—not because they are unqualified, but because no company would ever delegate such critical tasks to someone who isn't a full-time staffer. To be honest, the best way to learn how to have a job is, well, to start having one. Remember the first time you had sex? A job is sort of like that: you romanticize it, you fantasize about it, you're convinced that once you do it you're going to feel different and glamorous and important, and then . . . eh. But luckily your career, like your sex life, will improve. It just takes some practice.

The first thing you need to know is the difference between a job and a career. A job is something you do to get money and pay your bills. A *career* is the overall path that your working life takes. You should be more focused on the latter than the former. Do not walk into your first job expecting it to be your ideal career—a career is something you have to work toward. If your ideal career is to be a magazine editor, your first job might be as an editorial assistant, which means that you're more likely to answer an editor's phone than to set up a celebrity photo shoot or come up with clever headlines for the cover. You can't allow yourself to be bummed about the fact that you haven't immediately gone from ambitious college student to editor in chief of *Cosmo*. That just doesn't happen. The way to get through the darkest days at an assistant job is to think about how that gig, in some way, is getting you closer to that career you want to have. It may be something small, like teaching you a skill that will be useful when you get to the top of the ladder, or it may be something key like working at your dream company in an administrative position instead of an executive one. But the bottom line is that every job you have now is vital toward shaping the career you will have someday. So don't take it for granted. In this chapter, we'll talk a little bit about how you can make the best out of even the suckiest job— after all, if you hate the job you currently have, you want to find the best next job you possibly can.

The writer Barbara Kingsolver addressed this notion of job versus career, as well as the state of depression many liberal arts graduates face upon being told that their degrees or areas of study are "worthless" and that they now need to "grow up" and think more about money. In a 2008 commencement speech at Duke University, she said:

> Exhaled by culture, taken in like oxygen, we hold these truths to be self-evident: you get what you pay for. Success is everything. Work is what you do for money, and that's what counts. How could it be otherwise? And the converse of that last rule, of course, is that if you're not paid to do something, it can't be important. If a child writes a poem and proudly reads it, adults may wink and ask "Think there's a lot of money in that?" You may also hear this when you declare a major in English, or are being a good neighbor, or are

raising children: the road to "success" is not paved
with the likes of these.

In other words, being an assistant is not just about being
an assistant. It's about keeping you afloat financially and
being able to support yourself while also living your
dream—whether that's getting promoted into a job where
you make a lot more money, working on an artistic side
project like a band or the Great American Novel, or just
never needing to ask your parents for cash ever again.
But, ultimately, letting your job be the only thing that
defines you is a dangerous prospect. Whether it involves
having a hobby, being a volunteer, participating in a community activity, having a family, or doing anything else,
you need to have a healthy life outside of work, or you
can never have a healthy life at work.

Your assistant job may seem—and probably is—
pretty damn overwhelming. So here are a couple of things
you should do immediately in order to get yourself as set
as possible.

Learn *everybody*'s name—and, more important, exactly
what they do.

You will survive being an assistant only if you have
allies in the office. They may be other, more senior, assistants, but they might also be people in other departments or tertiary characters (like clients, contractors, or

people who have some connection to the company but don't actually work there). Get to know as many people as possible as quickly as you can. If it helps, make a map of your office with people's names labeled according to where they sit.

Learning names is step one—but learning what people do is a much more critical step two. I don't mean memorizing peoples' titles—I mean learning exactly what projects and tasks they're responsible for and what skills they're known for in the office. For example, knowing exactly who is in charge of things like payroll and health insurance benefits is super-important, because if you make friends with these people they will be a million times more likely to help you figure out your ridiculously complicated health plan coverage or make sure you get paid on time.

As you'll soon learn, being an assistant means that you constantly have to think on your feet and handle all kinds of weird situations. If your boss starts screaming at you about finding him a nice place to make a lunch reservation, but you just moved to town three weeks ago and couldn't name an expensive restaurant if your life depended on it, you need to know ASAP which assistant was born and raised here and can immediately hook you up with restaurant suggestions that'll match your boss's palate and neighborhood preference. If the printer breaks down and starts making a weird noise halfway through finishing the printouts you need for your boss's huge

afternoon meeting, it will be tremendously useful if you
know which assistant has a knack for figuring out which
magic button will get the printer to calm down and return to normal. Otherwise, you will be making one hell
of a depressing emergency Kinko's run in your brand-new
shoes, and who wants to do that if she doesn't have to?

We'll get into more detail about good and bad coworkers in chapter three. You need to survive a couple of
weeks first.

Learn as much as you can about your company and your
boss. Do a thorough Google search—or even borrow
LexisNexis login info from your friend in grad school—
and learn what you can about the company's history,
founders, earnings, and the like. You might even pick up
some valuable information about past scandals, like law-
suits. You never know when this information will be useful, but it couldn't hurt to be as knowledgeable as possible
about what's going on in other parts of your company.
That way, if they're having financial trouble or someone
mysteriously got sent packing last week, you might have
some insight into what happened—or at least not be totally shocked if it ends up impacting you or your workload. Plus, it's just smart to know things like who founded
the company, if it's still doing the same kind of business
or if it grew/evolved into something else, and what the
company's biggest and most notable achievements are.

That's simply smart research. You don't want to be in a meeting and betray the fact that you've never heard of the company's most famous invention.

I'd also suggest Googling your boss, as well as (if you know his name—it's probably on all your mail) the person who had your job before you. Yeah, it's stalkerish, so do it on your home computer. But it couldn't hurt to find out whether he is now working in a better job within the same industry or if he had a nervous breakdown and moved to Guam. Speaking of which . . .

No matter what you do, do not fall into the trap of being compared to your predecessor. It doesn't matter if the person who had your job before you was Mother Teresa or the biggest fuckup who ever fucked up—you do not want to be compared to him or her. If anybody tries to introduce you as "the new Kim" on your first day, very confidently but carefully put your foot down—try laughing it off and saying, "However, I go by the name [your name]." There is nothing good that can come out of being seen as Your Predecessor 2.0. If Kim was all sunshine and light and magic pixie dust, your boss is going to resent you—no matter how well you do at your job—for having the audacity not to be her. If Kim was a whiny bitch who got fired because she used expletives in a meeting with board members, you'll want to do your part to erase any potential link between the two of you, stat.

THE BELEAGUERED
ASSISTANT PLAYLIST

Program your iPod with these songs—they'll make great listening for your ride home from a really brutal day at work.

Johnny Paycheck—"Take This Job and Shove It"
  (Duh.)
Dolly Parton—"9 to 5"
  (Obviously.)
They Might Be Giants—"Minimum Wage"
  (Basically, if you've never heard this song before,
  it's somebody yelling, "Minimum wage!" and
  then a whip-cracking sound and then some
  music. It's a conceptual art piece, really.)
Donna Summer—"She Works Hard for the Money"
  (Because seriously. You do.)
R.E.M.—"Exhuming McCarthy"
  (Makes fun of bougie businesspeople types.
  You know, like the ones you work with. Plus, it's
  really catchy.)
The Bangles—"Manic Monday"
  (If all the tedious parts of your get-ready-for-
  work routine were written by Prince and sung
  by Susanna Hoffs, they'd be a lot more interest-
  ing. And they'd rhyme.)

Loverboy—"Working for the Weekend"
(I'd recommend playing this only on Friday afternoons as you're skipping out of the office early, otherwise it'll remind you exactly how many hours and minutes it is until the weekend starts.)

The Boomtown Rats—"I Don't Like Mondays"
(So, this song is based on a true story about this teenage girl who went and shot some people and when they asked her why she did it she said, "I don't like Mondays." Honestly, who doesn't feel that way when they walk into work to start a new week? There's a Tori Amos cover of this song if you prefer your workplace horror-show music more on the morose side.)

Bob Dylan—"Maggie's Farm"
(He doesn't want to work on Maggie's farm, you don't want to hand wash your boss's delicates. If you're feeling particularly emphatic, upgrade to the Rage Against the Machine version.)

Belle and Sebastian—"Step into My Office, Baby"
(If only your boss were as cool, or as sultry.)

George Michael—"Freedom"
(Ever had the urge to set your office, along with your cool retro jacket and jukebox, on fire? While cavorting with supermodels? Well, then this is the tune for you.)

Public Enemy—"Fight the Power"
   (In case you weren't sure, your boss is the
   power, and you're the one fighting.)
John Lennon—"Working Class Hero"
   (If you still, deep down, believe your job is
   inherently noble or something and/or seek
   reassurance.)

Learn your acronyms! OSHA stands for Occupational Safety and Health Administration. "Occupational" means "related to your occupation"—i.e., your job. In other words, OSHA is the government agency in charge of making sure you're safe at work. You can find out more about them at osha.gov. You should also study up on HIPAA, the Health Insurance Portability and Accountability Act (check them out at hipaa.org). When you first start a job, you will learn about health and safety regulations—you may think stuff like that has more to do with jobs like construction and food preparation, but it relates to ordinary offices too. You will be given pamphlets about OSHA regulations or told where the posters with OSHA information are hanging up in the office, but I am willing to bet you'll just sign whatever you're asked to sign without reading any of that boring-looking text. (I did.) It's never a bad idea to brush up on the law—poke around those two Web sites, even if they're way less interesting than reading your friend's blog of her year teaching in Japan.

Be a total eager beaver, at least for a while. You can't immediately start off being a slacker at work, even if you become one eventually. The first couple of weeks, you should walk that fine line between super-assistant and super-annoying. As in: be willing to stay late if you made a mistake on something and want to fix it, but don't skip the all-assistant lunch just so you can feel good about yourself and lord over everyone else because you worked through your lunch hour. Get as adept as possible at doing the basic mechanics of your job—printing and collating documents, using your boss's nonsensical filing system, highlighting stuff on Excel spreadsheets—so that you can master them quickly and move on to (hopefully) something interesting.

Find a way to connect with people, especially useful or important people.

You never know what people are going to remember about you. The best way you can make sure people remember your name instead of "Mr. So-and-so's assistant" is to find one personal way to connect with them. Maybe you went to the same college or are from the same hometown—that's an easy way to quickly create a bond.

But with other people, you might have to press a little harder. Perhaps offer a compliment (but do so only if you genuinely like a person's sweater/haircut/taste in subway reading—don't just throw out platitudes or you'll look like a brownnoser) and then try to engage the person in conversation about the thing you've complimented. For example, if she follows up your "That's a really cute sweater" with a "Thanks, I got it at such-and-such store," you can segue into a conversation about your preferred choices of online sales. My friend Shannon started a new job at a nonprofit and realized pretty quickly that every Thursday morning was devoted to dissecting what had happened on the previous night's episode of *Lost*. So she Netflixed the DVDs of earlier seasons, got caught up, and was able to participate in the group chat session. By the end, she was more addicted to the show than some of her coworkers were, but, more important, she doesn't get left out of key social interactions. And it's just a TV show she had to commit to, not an entire new wardrobe.

Get your job description clarified as much as humanly possible.

This seems basic—you're hired for a job and then you do it, right? Wrong, wrong, wrong. There is nothing companies love more than hiring somebody to do a job and then totally changing the job description the day he or she shows up at work. Take this story, for example:

My first job was as a receptionist at a small company. Everybody there seemed so nice and welcoming. I couldn't believe the job had been available for so long. Then I came in to start working. That's when I started to realize why the position had been open—they'd "forgotten" to tell me that I was supposed to be an assistant in addition to being the receptionist. I was working for a guy who had gotten demoted, so he was being punished by having his assistant be only part-time. His response to the demotion was to act like nothing had happened and assume I was his full-time assistant, even when I had plenty of other front desk–related work to do. I'd be in the middle of signing for a huge delivery and he'd be screaming at me to get into his office so loudly the entire office could hear, including the UPS guy, who actually told me he felt sorry for me. When I finally quit, I tried as nicely as possible in my exit interview to suggest they "clarify the job position during the hiring process."

—Julia, New York City

Ask around and observe the other assistants: is it normal for assistants to do personal work for their bosses, or are you the only one who gets asked to pick up the boss's kids from school? Do assistants at your company typically make overtime cash coming in on the weekends, or are you expected to do it unpaid whenever you're asked? What the job actually involves might be very different from how it was sold to you, so be sure you know exactly what you're getting into. Or, at the very least, when you decide to stick up for yourself, you'd better know for damn sure what the office standards are—"None of the other assistants are ever asked to come to their boss's home on weekends and do housework, and I don't think you should be allowed to ask me" works only if you're 100 percent sure about the "no one else" part.

BUZZWORD: THE COMBO JOB

When two positions (usually administrative) get combined into one sucky, underpaid, too-much-for-one-person job. Common examples include the office manager/assistant and the receptionist/assistant. Almost always, the combo job is created by someone tasked with saving money for the company and who thinks that admin jobs are "easy." Invariably, the combo job creator is rewarded for his or her innovation while the combo job holder is busy ordering lunch for the entire company, figuring out how payroll was two cents off last month, and updating his or her boss's list of contacts all at the same time.

. . .

On that note . . . it's time to brush up on your workplace law. This might sound extreme, but I suggest keeping a small notebook and jotting down anything you are asked to do that seems unusual or atypical. That could be anything from shredding documents to learning confidential information to being asked to rat out a coworker who's suspected of doing something against company policy. If you know a lawyer or other qualified person you can ask, check in with them about some of the stuff you've done or been asked to do at work. If you don't know anyone or don't feel comfortable asking about it, you can check out Web sites like workplacefairness.org or dol.gov (the U.S. Department of Labor's official site). It's up to you to decide how to act if you find out you're being asked to do something illegal or unethical. Many of the assistants who write into STA say that they know they are doing things that are against the law or that make them feel personally uncomfortable, but they don't feel that they're in a position to quit their jobs. They may not be financially secure enough to do so, or perhaps this job is their one chance to break into a super-competitive industry like fashion or finance. Whatever your motivations for deciding if you're going to stay at your job or go, continue keeping notes.

The New York–based media gossip Web site Gawker once reported a horror story about the Devil in Prada herself, Anna Wintour. Wintour had apparently insisted that a *Vogue* assistant cut her Rapunzel-length hair to a shoulder-grazing bob. The girl did so without question. Is this story humiliating? Yes. Illegal? Doubtful. Is it relevant to the assistant's job performance? Unlikely. But, the bottom line is, she did it. She didn't quit or say no or go complain to HR—instead, she went and got a haircut immediately. Why? Well, having a crazy demanding job can do odd things to people, including killing their self-esteem and making them feel trapped and subject to the whims of a narcissistic, demanding boss. Or it's possible that the assistant felt she might get fired if she refused to comply. Who knows? This kind of story is far from rare. STA readers have reported doing stuff beyond the call of duty while working as an assistant: picking up their boss's birth control (and going and getting a special "below the belt" ointment when said boss came down with a little infection), lying to their boss's wife—and his mistress, babysitting their boss's children, and picking out the boss's girlfriend's engagement ring.

BUZZWORD: DONNAWORK

Let's say your boss is a dude. And let's say your male boss has a wife, and her name is Donna. Invariably, while you are being paid only to do grunt work for your boss, you have unwittingly also become Donna's personal servant. This means that in addition to your actual work-related duties, you also have to make Donna's dermatologist appointments, remind her to pay the nanny, teach her how to check her voice mail, and renew her subscription to *Redbook* because she finds all those little reminder cards to be "so horribly confusing."

Do as much organizing/personalizing as you can now. Sad but true: when you get into the thick of your job (basically, as soon as you aren't able to get away with "Oh, I'm new" as a perma-excuse) you will never have as much time to yourself as you'd like. Such is the nature of being an assistant: you're usually making laps around the office all day, doing your part to wear down the carpet between your boss's office and the reception desk, the copier, the break room, and your desk. If you want to post cute photos of you and your family from that cruise you took last Christmas, do it now, or your cubicle walls might remain bare forever. If you decorate your cube during your first week, it looks like you're getting settled. If you do it any time after that, it looks like you're just screwing around and wasting time. Keep in mind that having personal, meaningful objects in your work space is a good way to remind you of what's really important and to prevent you from getting too stressed. That said, don't make it *too* personal: your desk is not your bedroom. Tasteful photos (none of you in Señor Frog's doing tequila shots, none involving PDA), some souvenirs (concert or movie ticket stubs are fine, but maybe not Mardi Gras beads), or plants and flowers are appropriate. As for your collection of Beanie Babies? I'd leave those at home.

If you have a particular organization system you like, get it implemented as soon as you can. The more of an infrastructure you have in place, the better, and it'll be really helpful once the work starts to pile up. Find out where the storage room/supply closet is and raid it. If you want folders, get folders. If you write everything down on Post-its, get Post-its. At my assistant job I had a mini office stashed under my desk. Since I was often chained to my desk for long stretches at a time, not able to get up and do anything in case the phone rang, I learned pretty quickly that it was incredibly useful to keep extra staples, pens, company stationery, Wite-Out, and paper clips within grabbing distance at all times. You can replenish when you have down time, but always err on the side of your cube looking like an office supply store.

Also, if you have any personal essentials—basically, anything you always keep in your backpack, purse, or glove compartment—that you can't get in the office, be sure to keep a stash with you. Popular assistant "extras" include lotion, hand sanitizer, gum, breath mints, hair elastics, a backup cell phone charger, tampons, a sewing kit, a contact lens case and solution, a toothbrush and toothpaste, and perfume or cologne. After all, you spend (at least) forty hours a week in your office—it really is your home away from home, and you never know what sanitary or household items you will want or need. And if you're stuck at your desk or at least not able to leave the office for hours at a time, it couldn't hurt to have basics around for yourself or other assistants. I even kept clothes at my desk—I had a nice sweater that I could put on over my outfit if I ended up going out after work and didn't have time to go home and change, plus some stuff I could wear to the gym if I'd forgotten to bring my yoga bag that day. Within a week at my first job, I knew which assistants could be counted on to supply me with junk food if I was low on energy or who would have clear nail polish if I tore my tights. And, of course, I returned the favor and was happy to let anyone use one of the five kinds of lip balm I always had at the ready.

While you're at it, make a "babysitter list." This is a list of important people in the office and in your boss's life, the equivalent of the list of emergency contact numbers that parents leave tacked to the refrigerator door when someone's babysitting their kids. Their list includes the pediatrician and Grandma; the one you make should be a little more formal. Include shortcuts for people in the office who you talk to a lot or need to communicate with often, plus your boss's home number, contact info for the boss's family members, the land line for his country house, and home and cell numbers for his business partners, associates, and/or clients. Of course, you'll have some kind of system, like Lotus or Microsoft Outlook, that lets you store tons of similar information online. The babysitter list should be only the most essential and frequently called numbers. If that includes something unsavory like the number for his dealer or his mistress, try to come up with an innocuous code name. In time, you'll probably have all this information committed to memory (true story: I still know the home and cell number for my boss from five years ago), but the temp who has to fill in for you when you go on vacation will be eternally grateful for the cheat sheet you've provided.

BUZZWORD: OFFICE PLAGUE

The sickness you get upon starting a new job, when you have to adjust your body to the particular germs of your new office. Can also be defined as the phenomenon that happens when one person in the office gets sick but insists on coming to work anyway so that they can (a.) look like a mar-

tyr, and (b.) save their actual sick days for, like, going to Burning Man; this selfish person then infects
the entire office.

If you're a second assistant, become BFF with the first
assistant. In *The Devil Wears Prada*, Anne Hathaway gets
hired to be the second assistant to Meryl Streep's evil
boss character. Immediately, she learns the ropes from
Emily Blunt's character, who is the first—aka senior—
assistant. If you are a second assistant to someone, the
first assistant is the number-one person you need to befriend. She has been working for this person already and
can provide help and insight on everything from your
boss's pet peeves to office protocol. The first assistant is
your absolute best resource. Unfortunately, plenty of first
assistants get power trippy from having someone (that
would be you) to boss around. Be sure to be nice and
complimentary—but *not* a doormat. Remember the dis-
tinction: you are your boss's second assistant, not the first
assistant's first assistant.

Here's one of the most horrifying second assistant
stories I have ever heard. If something like this happens
to you, you should seriously begin considering other
options. Or just leaving and going home. I wouldn't judge
you.

I should have known things would go horribly wrong when on my first day of work my new boss introduced me around as her SECOND assistant. I have no problems working as someone's second assistant to a busy/important person, but she DIDN'T HAVE a first assistant. When I questioned her about this, she told me I wasn't qualified to do the job—regardless of my previous experience and prestigious university degree. This was just a way to degrade whoever sat in the chair outside her office. This sentiment was reinforced by her comment of "The only reason I hired you was to have a warm body outside my office."

After months of verbal abuse that included insulting my intelligence, appearance, personality, and ideas I was reduced to a quivering ball of nerves that started vomiting in the morning and smoking on my lunch breaks (I hadn't been a smoker before this job). The cherry on the sundae was during Christmas she would give gifts to her staff. She would parade us into the conference room and make us watch each of us open the gifts she would personally select. You would know where you stood in the pecking order based on the price/quality of a gift. You could receive designer clothes or something she found in the bottom of her purse. When it was finally my turn, I opened my gift—a cute bag filled with designer cosmetics. I was ecstatic because I had thought she was rewarding me for all of my hard work and tolerance of her abuse.

I enthusiastically thanked her for such a nice gift and, much like kidnap victims suffering from Stockholm syndrome, I was ready to forgive her heinous behavior. After we had left the conference room, a colleague informed me that she had told them that my gift was in fact the FREE gift with purchase she had received when buying an expensive new line of cosmetics for her daughter. In her estimation, I wasn't even worth buying a gift for and she made sure that everyone in the company knew.

Soon after, I left that job, but have heard that she still has a constant stream of assistants because no one is good enough to be her first, second, or third assistant.

—Jessica, New York City

Make a budget. You'll find out very quickly that your salary is different from the amount of cash you actually take home every week. I can tell you from personal experience that it is seriously fucking depressing to look at your first paycheck expecting to see a certain amount and then realizing you end up with less than that thanks to that awesome "now you're a grown-up and get to pay five kinds of taxes" reality.

So, it's time to crunch some numbers. Yeah, I know, after that first-semester-of-college math class, you thought you'd never have to bust out the calculator again, but you're going to have to do some real-world math. Now that you know how much you clear per paycheck, you can figure out about how much you can afford for rent, food, utilities—and other equally important essentials, like vodka, concert tickets, and shoes. Oh, and if you don't have a savings account? Get one. While I was an assistant, I put every extra quarter I could in my savings account, which I referred to as my "take this job and shove it" fund. Even if you feel pretty happy with or secure at your job, it can never hurt to have some extra cash lying around. Whether you use it to go on a much-needed vacation or hold on to it in case you get laid off is up to you. If math isn't your favorite thing, you might want to download a personal-finance software system like Quicken or sign up for a free online organizational service like Remember the Milk.

BUZZWORD: MORALE

Something that is talked about only when it does not exist. If a recruiter or HR person tells you in an interview that the company has "high morale," it usually means exactly the opposite. Any company that throws, sponsors, or organizes events with "morale" or "morale-boosting" in the title is most likely doing so because all their employees are miserable. No one throws morale-boosting events for happy employees—they just have parties.

In his wryly funny novel about the modern workplace, *Personal Days*, Ed Park writes, "Morale has been low since the Firings began last year. Pru says *morale* is a word thrown around only in the context of its absence. You never look at a hot young thing and say, *check out that spring chicken*, but only use it to describe your great-aunt: *she's no spring chicken*."

Figure out what kind of leverage, if any, you might have. If you have a boss or higher-up who is always giving you annoying projects to work on or constantly breathing down your neck about deadlines, you will still have to smile and be all "I'd *love* to help you!" Sucks, but it's true. If your office were McDonald's, you'd be the cashier and he'd be the customer—in other words, he is always right, even if he's wrong. So how can you deal with the insane workload being hurled at your head, and the snide way any comment gets delivered? I'm not telling you to go all renegade or anything, but trust that workplace karma *always* comes back around sooner or later.

Here's the thing about being somebody's assistant— you have almost total access to his or her life. If you're a personal assistant, you most likely know your boss's PIN, social security number, credit card info, e-mail password, and more. Essentially, you're a more disgruntled and more badly compensated extension of your boss. While it means you often get treated like you're invisible, it has some advantages. You should never voice threats or make your boss aware that you know about his mistress—blackmail is illegal, and you're better than that. But he knows you know. Here's an example of one way an assistant turned a negative work situation around when she learned something about her boss's proclivities:

I'm a junior editor at a newspaper. My friend and I are the two newest junior editors, so we always get stuck working on "Editor X"'s stupid projects. Editor X is this boring, kind of plodding guy who is a higher-up at the paper. For some reason everyone continues to think that he's really important, but everyone manages to weasel out of working with him because all his projects are time-consuming and no one ever reads them. Once, after making my friend and me turn around a story overnight with practically no help, he had the audacity to tell our managing editor that my friend and I were slackers.

It took a while, but finally my friend and I got a break. One night the friend and I were both stuck late at the office working on yet another Editor X project. When my friend went by X's office to show him some edits, he busted X (a devoted family man) watching porn on his computer! My friend never

said anything, but X definitely knew about it. Since
then, my friend and I have not been assigned to work
on a single one of X's stories, and X can't look either of
us in the eye anymore, especially when his wife and
adorable children show up unannounced at the office.
—*Daisy, New York City*

I doubt that Daisy ever said anything to her boss about
what happened that night—it sounds like she was as
mortified as he was. However, the fact that her boss was
well aware that she knew something bad about him may
have caused him to behave better around her or at least
realize he'd been inappropriate and needed to clean up
his act in the future. I'm willing to bet that their boss/
assistant relationship improved after that fateful night.

Choose your mantra. A mantra is a word or phrase you
repeat multiple times to relax yourself. If you've ever
taken yoga classes, you might be familiar with mantras
like "Om shanti om," which everyone in the class repeats
over and over again as a way to calm down and clear their
minds before beginning the class. To be totally honest
with you, it is almost a given that sooner or later something at your job will result in your hiding in a bathroom
stall and crying. It could be something big and obvious
like your boss yelling at you and calling you horrible
names, or it could just be a lot of frustration and anxiety

wearing you down over time until you finally crack. Either way, you will feel embarrassed about your crying, despite the fact that everyone in your office has probably done the same thing themselves. So, come up with a mantra you can chant at trying times like those. Some popular suggestions from STA readers include:

- This job is not my life.
- Tomorrow is another day.
- Breathe, breathe, breathe.
- Don't take it personally.
- This too shall pass.
- I will rise above this. I am better than this.
- Let it go, let it go, let it go.

I know we've just covered a ton of information, from office supplies to workplace karma to financial planning. It may seem totally overwhelming. However, you've just entered a new phase in your life and, like any phase, it takes adjustment. You may not have realized during your first week of college that you were actually learning way more than statistics and geology—like, how to cook using a hot plate, how to live with a weird or annoying roommate in a tiny space with no privacy, and which bars will let you in without checking ID—even if you didn't notice. Trust that the more work you do now, the less you'll have to do later.

QUIZ
What TV Assistant Are You?

1. You feel happiest at work when:
    a. Your boss finally recognizes one of your accomplishments.
    b. Everybody is happy and nothing is going wrong.
    c. The cute coworker you have a crush on invites you to lunch.
    d. Nobody throws anything at your head for an entire day.
    e. Your boss doesn't do anything illegal that you would have had to take the rap for.

2. Do you get dressed up to go to work?
    a. I just wear what I would normally wear—I value myself based on achievements, not looks.
    b. Yes, of course! A uniform isn't complete without a big smile.
    c. I try to look nice, but stick to conservative clothes so I don't stand out too much.
    d. Suits or nothing for me. After all, you're supposed to dress for the job you want, not the job you have, right?
    e. Once I found an appropriate work outfit, I decided to wear it every single day.

3. Would you ever drink alcohol at the office?
   a. Only if my boss was drinking and offered me
      some—I wouldn't want to be rude.
   b. Never. I don't even like drinking coffee at work . . .
      it makes me tense.
   c. Not every day, but I don't think there's anything
      wrong with some margaritas at the office party
      when you're trying to get everybody to loosen up.
   d. I keep a flask in my desk drawer.
   e. Only if I got fired and needed to drink the pain away.

4. How long do you see yourself remaining at your
   current job?
   a. Not too long—I'm a go-getter and really want to
      get promoted.
   b. As long as everybody's happy with my work, why
      rock the boat?
   c. I often say I'm going to quit soon, but my life keeps
      getting in the way.
   d. The fact that I keep coming in every day is a miracle,
      to be honest.
   e. This is my dream job. I'm staying forever.

5. Have you ever considered hooking up with your boss?
   a. No, although I think other people think we should
      get together.
   b. Only if I was under orders, because I hate saying no.
   c. Hooking up with your boss is against HR policy, and

I wouldn't want to lose my job. Hooking up with a
coworker, though . . .

   d. Never. My boss is not my type.

   e. Every day.

6. What is the most embarrassing thing you've ever had
   to do at work?
   a. Handle personal disputes between my boss and
      his family members.
   b. Thankless busywork and errand-running—
      sometimes to another state.
   c. Make amends for my boss, who got drunk and
      ruined an important meeting.
   d. Get down on my hands and knees and grovel for
      my job.
   e. Do things that compromised my beliefs or went
      against my values.

7. Does your boss know anything about your personal life?
   a. Yes, we often discuss our problems with each
      other and give each other advice.
   b. I don't really have much of a life outside of work,
      so it's not an issue.
   c. I try not to talk about it too much, but I feel like I
      have to share personal details if my boss keeps
      asking.
   d. Yes, and he uses that information to guilt me or
      emotionally abuse me.

    e. No. I basically exist only to work for him, and he doesn't think about me otherwise.

8.   What is your work weakness?
   a. I take everything too personally and have trouble separating my work and my life.
   b. I try too hard to please everyone.
   c. I let myself get in a rut and have a hard time getting out.
   d. I have a passive-aggressive relationship with my boss.
   e. I'm a perfectionist and my own harshest critic.

MOSTLY As: You are Betty Suarez.

Beautiful-on-the-inside Betty was a hardworking girl from Queens who held her own against snobby colleagues at superglam *Mode* magazine on the ABC sitcom *Ugly Betty*. Rather than try to impress people with expensive clothes, Betty believed in working hard and getting ahead the old-fashioned way. Although she sometimes had to deal with setbacks, she managed to balance her work and home life pretty successfully, and won the respect of her boss for her ability to think on her feet.

MOSTLY Bs: You are Kenneth Parcell.

Kenneth came all the way from rural Georgia to work as an NBC page on the show-within-a-show *30 Rock* in Manhattan. All alone in the big city, Kenneth has made his office his home, befriending his coworkers and taking on extra work whenever he gets the chance. Unfortunately, he sometimes gets pulled into the drama of his coworkers' personal lives, but somehow Kenneth always manages to teach people life lessons and make them realize their errors.

MOSTLY Cs: You are Pam Beesly.

The Office's receptionist with the mostest manages to remain calm in even the most absurd of circumstances. She's the one who gets called on to settle bets, resolve disputes, and dispense life advice. Sometimes, though, her coworkers take her "Office Sweetheart" persona a bit too far and assume she's a doormat.

MOSTLY Ds: You are Lloyd Lee.

As the assistant to big-shot Hollywood talent agent Ari Gold on HBO's *Entourage*, Lloyd's daily duties involved everything from making phone calls and setting up meetings to sabotaging rival agents and hanging out with the occasional celebrity client. While Lloyd took a lot of grief (emotional blackmail, physical abuse, homophobia) from his devilish, bombastic boss, he was definitely not a pawn—he knew how to utilize the "assistant mafia" in order to make friends and win favors. Lest you think Lloyd's promotion means he's out of the woods forever, he's now competing against his former boss—and using all the same dirty tricks.

MOSTLY Es: You are Waylon Smithers.

The greatest cartoon assistant ever works as evil billionaire Mr. Burns's right-hand man on Fox's stalwart series *The*

Simpsons. However, he's more involved than the average assistant, even living with and working as the occasional nursemaid for his decrepit boss. Smithers's devotion is so boundless that he even helps Burns to carry out plans that Smithers finds morally or ethically repugnant. When we do get glimpses of his nonwork life, though, he seems like a pretty decent dude, albeit one with a slightly unhealthy appreciation for dolls.

TWO

Bosses: The Bad, the Ugly, and the (Rarely) Good

You hate your job? Oh, why didn't you say so?
There's a club for that. It's called EVERYBODY,
and we meet at the bar.

—*The Drew Carey Show*

How, you might be wondering, does a bad boss get that way? Just as we examine what compels a serial killer to kill people, we should take a close look at the characteristics of a bad boss and use them to help us figure out how he or she got that way. Perhaps they had sad childhoods. Perhaps they're sociopaths.

After all, once *The Devil Wears Prada* outed Anna Wintour as an evil boss to people who previously hadn't even heard of her or looked at a single issue of *Vogue* magazine in their entire lives, why does she continue to have a job—and a constant stream of people who desperately want to be her assistant?

One word: "money." Bosses usually become bosses because they do something that brings in money, whether that's being a kick-ass fund-raiser, bringing in wealthy clients, or producing a monthly magazine that gets stellar ad rates. Let's do some quick math here, shall we? Suppose that Boss A is responsible for bringing twenty million dollars of revenue a year into the company, before taxes. For this, they get 15 percent commission, or three million bucks. So the company makes about seventeen million dollars a year from Boss A. Boss A has an assistant. We'll call her Assistant B. This assistant earns $30,000 a year. Now let's suppose that Boss A and Assistant B hate each other and can't work together harmoniously. Their massive hate of each other is getting in the way of doing their work and—the most important thing—making money. The company has to fire one of the two people. Which one do you think it will be? I'll give you a hint: it's not the one responsible for bringing in seventeen million dollars.

There's a truth that you can apply not only to bad bosses, but to bad employees: most bosses don't think they're bad. They have detached from reality, are surrounded by sycophants who tell them how awesome they are, or simply have never been called to task for their misdeeds. Most of us have trouble seeing ourselves as others see us, and bad bosses often lack self-awareness. My former boss not only thought he wasn't a bad boss, he never missed a chance to tell me how great he thought he was: if he "let" me take a half day on a day when the office was going to close at one p.m. anyway, he would make sure to stop by my desk a couple times to remind me how nice it was of him to allow me to leave early. Evil bosses love to talk about how benevolent they are, and they also love to make any situation sound like the assistant's fault instead of theirs. I cannot tell you how many times executives have told me their biggest issue at work is that they're "too nice" to their assistants—maybe it's true occasionally, but those bosses would be the overwhelming exception. A good rule of thumb is to assume that the more a boss talks about how kind and loving she is, the worse she probably is to work for. It's a case of "the lady doth protest too much." Have you ever noticed how, when the halves of a celebrity couple won't shut up about how they're all in love with each other and they're so happy spending time together and blah blah blah rainbows and kittens, they always get divorced like a month later?

As long as Anna Wintour keeps producing and selling copies of *Vogue* that include 114 pages' worth of ads, she will continue to have a job. And as long as she continues to have a job that's possibly the most prestigious in the fashion industry, she will always have people willing to put up with working for her if they think it'll help them land their dream job someday. When people become successful, they get rewarded for it. Some bosses want luxury cars or a private jet so they don't have to travel with the common folk. Some bosses want catered lunch every day so they don't have to stop working. Whatever it is, once a person gets used to a standard of living he, well, *gets used to it.* Meaning, if your boss has had breakfast in bed every single day for twenty years, she is going to be pretty confused—and likely pissed off—if delivery stops one day. So you'd better hope you're not the one who has to stop delivering.

THE BOSSARY

A GLOSSARY OF BAD BOSSES

If Tolstoy had been an assistant, he might have said that all good bosses are alike, but all bad bosses are different in their own way. I know that every evil boss is evil in his own special way, but in this section we identify several of the most common types. This will help you to spot a bad boss earlier (perhaps even when you're interviewing for the job) and give you tips on how to handle one if it's too late to cut and run.

THE NON-SPOUSE

He's married to his job, and by default he's also married to you. He tells you how to dress, expects you to pick up his dry cleaning, and asks you for dating tips when he "gets back into the game." It usually isn't until he calls your parents' house in the middle of Thanksgiving dinner wanting to know where you put his favorite fountain pen that you realize you're a spouse instead of an employee.

The Non-spouse

The non-spouse is unable to make distinctions between his work and his life. As a result, he's usually successful in his chosen profession, but he's probably a workaholic. Because of the inability to separate job and life, his closest friends are his coworkers and business associates. If he's married, his spouse is probably someone he met through work or his college sweetheart who is okay with always being second to his job. More likely, though, he's divorced, because he cared more about working than spending time at home.

WHAT HE WEARS: Generic business wear. He's not one to bust out anything crazy like a brown suit or a tie with any nonstripe design.

WHAT HE DRINKS: At work, black coffee. During his three-martini lunch? Three martinis. No kidding.

FAMOUS EXAMPLE: Hugh Grant as George Wade in *Two Weeks Notice* (but not interesting or hot, or anybody you'd actually date).

HOW TO COPE: Set your boundaries *early*. That means when you say no, be really clear about meaning no. Turn your cell phone off on weekends. Don't give him a way to contact you when you're on vacation. If you've already broken this barrier, think of some kind of outside scenario that would (a.) take up a lot of time, and (b.) isn't something you could get in trouble for. Something like a sick relative is perfect. It sucks to have to lie about something like that, but "Sorry, I can't do that because I have to go take care of my sick relative" is such a good line that it essentially trumps any "I need you to do X" conversation.

BUZZWORD: CUBICLE SPEED

Anything that helps you to stay awake and alert at the office—or, if you're hungover, just helps you survive the day long enough to go home and pass out. Popular forms of cubicle speed include coffee, Red Bull, chocolate, caffeine pills, and self-loathing.

THE FRENEMY

Initially, she tries to be your best friend. She compliments your hair color and clothing. She wants to know all about your personal life and tells you all about hers in kind, usually over drinks—lots of drinks. One day though, just when you think you might be getting somewhere professionally, she does an about-face. You're a threat, unless she needs you as a scapegoat for some kind of transgression—but that usually comes after you've been sacked.

WHAT SHE WEARS: Whatever *Vogue* says is currently in style, or a lesser-priced knockoff that she bought in Chinatown or at Forever 21 and dresses up with expensive accessories. After a couple months in her employ, she wears exact replicas of your favorite outfit.

WHAT SHE DRINKS: Grande low-fat no-foam frappuccinos with green straws, not black ones. After work, it's all about the ultragirly pink Cosmopolitan.

FAMOUS EXAMPLE: Michael Douglas as Gordon Gekko in *Wall Street*.

The Frenemy

HOW TO COPE: The less you give the Frenemy to work with, the less she can use against you. Even though she might try to engage you in conversation, be careful not to rise to the bait. Be deliberately vague when asked outright questions: if she wants to know where you got that adorable new jacket, tell her it was a gift or that you got it at a thrift shop. If she asks what you're doing this weekend, tell her you're going to stay home and read a book. The Frenemy is a bit like a mosquito, and if your blood isn't easily accessible, she'll probably buzz off and try to find someone else's veins.

If you have trouble not responding to her questions or would rather just give her an answer than let her get all defensive, try to throw her off track by claiming to love certain stores/designers/bands just to see if she'll try to copy you. At the very least, it could be an interesting social experiment and bring back some memories of middle school.

BUZZWORD: THE CYA FILE

CYA, or "Covering Your Ass," is an incredibly important aspect of any job. You never know when someone is going to try to sabotage you or get you fired, so the best thing you can do in your own defense is keep an ongoing file of things that make you look good. Possible items in the CYA File can include praise-filled e-mails from your boss, coworkers, or outside clients/vendors, positive annual reviews, any good press the company gets that quotes you or specifically mentions an event/program/initiative you spearheaded, and any awards or recognitions you got from the company. Maybe someday you'll have to pull out the CYA File in response to an ambush when you ask for a raise.

THE BOSS'S KID

You probably went to a better school than him. You definitely have a higher IQ than him. But because of his good luck at being born into the right family, he gets to sit in his fancy desk chair and tell you what to do. Like plan his golfing trip in California. Or put his family heirlooms up for auction on eBay. Whatever it is, you're not learning anything, but you can't piss him off for fear of never working in this town again.

The Boss's Kid

WHAT HE WEARS: Something totally against dress code, like denim cutoffs or cargo pants, because no one will ever say anything to him about it.

WHAT HE DRINKS: Top-shelf expensive scotch. The stuff you can't get at a bar.

FAMOUS EXAMPLE: Eric Mabius as Daniel Meade on *Ugly Betty*.

HOW TO COPE: Plenty of Boss's Kids aren't intrinsically bad people—they're often just spoiled and have a skewed view of reality. It wouldn't hurt to occasionally mention your own poverty-level conditions the next time BK goes off about his luxurious vacation. Don't seek pity, but when he asks if you'd recommend Barbados or Bermuda, tell him honestly that the last time you went on a vacation it was to your mom's house. Sprinkle the occasional down-to-earth comment throughout and it might help BK realize how the other half lives. Or, perhaps, he'll give you a handout because he feels bad.

Also, try to—in a low-key way—jump on your boss's connections. He probably went to prep school with people who have amazing jobs now, and BK is your ticket to getting to know them. Be careful and don't make it look like you're taking advantage of your boss, but make sure you're in good with the assistants of the cronies in his A-list circle.

THE OVERSTRESSER

With this boss, you never know what's really important, because he flips out about everything. He treats the grocery store not having his favorite coffee filters with the same amount of panic as a major client threatening to leave the company. Every day is a nonstop stress party when this boss is around, and you find his anxiety rubbing off on you to the point where you're losing your hair.

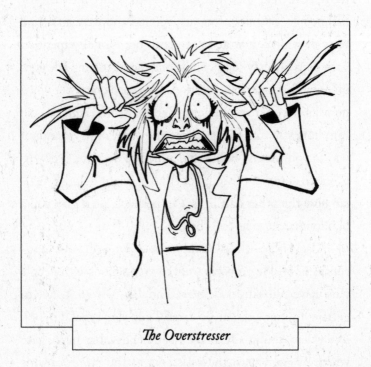

The Overstresser

WHAT HE WEARS: An impeccable suit, complete with matching pocket square. For women, it's the same, with a flawless manicure and antique pearls.

WHAT HE DRINKS: About fourteen cups of coffee a day, which ought to help explain those jitters. Sometimes the java washes down a handful of Xanax.

FAMOUS EXAMPLE: Jeremy Piven playing Ari Gold on *Entourage*, who makes screaming a fine art.

HOW TO COPE: Paxil. If you don't have a prescription, try Zen meditation.

No, seriously. The best way to counter an Overstresser is to be painfully calm. If you get tense and start yelling too, it turns into a shouting contest. The louder his voice gets, the quieter yours should be. If he shouts a question at you, he'll be forced to lower his own voice in order to hear you.

It also helps to have something to shoot back anytime the Overstresser is on a tear about something. I'm not saying you should turn into your mom and invoke poor starving orphans in Bangladesh in order to make your boss feel guilty for bitching about those missing tomatoes on his sandwich, but if you have quick and pertinent responses to all of his complaints it might help nip things in the bud. For example, if he's flipping out about his favorite restaurant not having a table open for lunch, be armed with several suggestions of other restaurants he might want to try, complete with reminders like "No, remember, you told me you loved that place. You had the veal piccata and talked about it for two days. The maître d's name is Vincenzo. I can call him for you." Overstressers tend to be the kind of people who channel all their energy into freaking out about a problem rather than actually fixing it, so if you provide solutions, it might calm them down or at least stop their panicking for a minute.

BUZZWORD: BOSS IT UP

To act like a jerk (aka your boss), but ideally with some kind of specific purpose. For example, if the person who was supposed to send you sales figures you asked for a week ago is not responding to your e-mails and your boss asks you about it every fifteen minutes to the point where you might go postal, you might decide to boss it up a little, march over to Sales Figure Guy's desk, and be a giant asshole to him—not taking "no" for an answer, insisting he drop whatever he's working on and help you now—until he gives you what you want. People may be afraid of your boss, but they also do what he wants immediately in order to get rid of him.

The opposite of this strategy is to play up one's beleagueredness. By acting as if you are even more sleep-deprived and miserable than you already are, you may get a person to help you out of sheer pity.

THE PTP (PAST THEIR PRIME)

Working for this person will open tons of doors for you in the industry—if you're sixty-five. This boss used to be a hotshot, but now he has no real projects to work on and gets stuck in a corner office because everyone at the company is too scared to force him to retire. Instead of getting hands-on experience in your field, you get to bring him coffee six times a day while he lectures you about how this business just doesn't have *integrity* anymore.

WHAT HE WEARS: A suit that was the absolute last word in style—about fifteen years ago. It also probably smells like it's been hanging in the closet surrounded by mothballs ever since.

WHAT HE DRINKS: He doesn't need none of this fancy Starbucks shit, oh no, he remembers back when coffee was just *coffee*, damn it.

FAMOUS EXAMPLE: Martin Landau as Bob Ryan on *Entourage*.

The PTP
(PAST THEIR PRIME)

HOW TO COPE: Humor the guy a bit. Let him think that you really are sending telegrams when you're actually shooting off e-mails—what he doesn't know won't hurt him. Furthermore, you won't have to hurt his ego, and he won't think of you as a stuck-up brat who likes to sass him. When he starts rambling about some story from years ago that you've heard a dozen times already, just smile and nod. Pretend he's your grandpa telling you that story about the war again.

Also, if you can, use his repeated meanderings as a chance to pick his brain. Even though the people he knows might no longer be in the business or useful to you as a contact, it couldn't hurt to know the back story of the industry you're in. You never know when a fact that you picked up from one of the PTP's interminable sermons about the way things used to be could really impress a future employer who thinks that all twenty-somethings believe the world didn't begin until the Internet was invented. Try to keep in mind some of your boss's past accomplishments so that when you interview for your next job you can sound reverential and like you see your boss as an asset instead of a relic.

THE FUNCTIONAL ILLITERATE

Your boss is "really good" at his job. Unfortunately, he's so good at his job that he's managed to get by all this time without knowing how to turn on his computer. It becomes your job to baby him, whether that means spending the first fifteen minutes of every day teaching him how to check his voice mail again or having to write everything manually since he can't figure out how to use MS Word. And I won't get started on how many times he sticks his ignorant foot in his ignorant mouth.

WHAT HE WEARS: He may have on a nice suit, but watch for the giant ink stain on his shirt pocket or the belt loop he missed in the back.

The Functional Illiterate

WHAT HE DRINKS: Coffee, with milk, although half of it ends up spilled on either his sport coat or his desk.

FAMOUS EXAMPLE: Gary Cole as Bill Lumbergh in *Office Space*.

HOW TO COPE: Being remotely competent at anything will immediately indicate to the rest of the company that you are a good employee compared to your numbskull of a boss. Just don't be *too* good, or he might catch on and make you do all his work for him. Truth is, you don't need to sit around plotting a detailed plan for corporate espionage when the FI will do most of the work for you. Why think up a complicated plot for making his presentation go horribly in front of the big boss, thereby exposing him as a total bonehead, when he's pretty likely to do that all by himself? Better to let your boss hang himself once in a while—just make sure your fingerprints are very, very far from the rope.

One downside of the FI is that you often spend so much time helping him with tasks that should be easy that you then have to work extra hard to do your *actual* work, like the girl in this horror story recounts:

> *My boss is an avid collector of memorabilia from a seventies rock band. He has a large collection of stuff to fill his empty life, stuff that sends him back to his glory days or whatever you want to call them. He also happens to be completely computer illiterate. This means that he constantly interrupts me in the middle of important tasks so that I can work on his collecting. The other day, while I was working on an important client-related task with an important deadline, my boss comes busting into my office and tells me he has a project that simply cannot wait. He hands me a tape and tells me to take care of it immediately. What, you ask, could be so important that he would ask me to drop everything? He had dictated a list of memorabilia*

he was purchasing to include with a check. It was apparently extremely urgent that I type it all up and then fill out a FedEx form for him. I ended up having to stay late that night and finish my real work.

—Roxy, Washington, D.C.

BUZZWORD: DINING AL DESKO

Eating lunch, or any other meal, at your desk while continuing to work. It may be a sandwich you brown-bagged to the office in order to be more fiscally responsible, or it may be something you went and picked up and then brought back to the office. Either way, it's depressing, and you should do it as rarely as possible. Sure, sometimes there's a huge backlog of stuff you have to get done and you just can't get away from your desk for even a second, but the reason lunch breaks exist isn't only so you can eat: it's so you can have some time away from working. Even if you brought in a sandwich, eat it in the park or grab a coworker friend and eat together in an empty conference room. Anything that gets your mind away from work for a while will make you more rational and focused when you go back.

THE DRAMA QUEEN

Sure, you can handle answering her phone, managing her calendar, and organizing her files. But it's never enough. Do you come in promptly at 8:59 every morning even though the front door isn't open till nine and you don't have keys? You slacker, come in by eight thirty. Is that a very very tiny stain on your blouse? Way to make the company look bad. And by the way, I need that grande triple nonfat cappuccino with extra foam *now*.

The Drama Queen

WHAT SHE WEARS: Something you could spend the rest of your life saving for and still not afford. Also, fur. Possibly from an animal she killed herself.

WHAT SHE DRINKS: Coffee is so last year. Now it's only herbal tea or vitaminwater. And don't ever make the mistake of thinking she eats.

FAMOUS EXAMPLE: The divine Meryl Streep as Miranda Priestly in *The Devil Wears Prada.*

HOW TO COPE: You are going to need a *big* support network. Have all the most useful people in the office on speed dial—the assistant who handles the CEO's meeting schedule, the guy who delivers the mail, the assistant who is always able to make the printer stop doing that weird thing where it says it's jammed but it isn't, and soon. Also, start building a network of people outside the office who can help you cope with whatever the diva needs. For example, if she has a hyperspecific, complicated cocktail order, make sure you're on a first-name basis with the workers at the two closest bars so that you can call ahead when she's on the way there to get drinks with an important client. The more streamlined you can make your process, the easier you can make your life. Sad as it sounds, sometimes it helps to play up your victim status in order to get things done. Never do this in front of your boss, of course, but if being pathetic and disheveled inspires the Starbucks barista to let you cut in line and get your boss's drink made more quickly, your continued sanity is an end that justifies the means. Go ahead, let people play the hero for you. Just don't ever forget that it's a temporary solution—you don't want to be in a permanent state of victimhood.

THE GHOSTMAKER

You're the eighth assistant she's had this year, so don't feel bad when you're assigned an e-mail address like "janesassistant@company.com." She ignores you at staff meetings, never says thank you, and has to be reminded of appointments multiple times because you're such a nonentity to her that she never listens to anything you say. The upside: she can't fire you if she doesn't remember your name.

WHAT SHE WEARS: The sweater her last assistant got her for her birthday. And no, she didn't send a thank-you note.

WHAT SHE DRINKS: The same exact beverage every day, although she will always be surprised when you hand it to her without having to ask what she'd like.

FAMOUS EXAMPLE: Mr. Burns on *The Simpsons*.

The Ghostmaker

HOW TO COPE: If she can't be bothered to learn your name, make it your mission to be sure everyone else knows you. Become BFF with the janitor, the receptionist, the CEO, the FedEx guy, and anybody else in sight range. If she's never going to recognize your accomplishments, you're going to have to make sure everyone else at the company does. Imagine how bad she'll look if the president of the company mentions something that you worked on and she actually says "Who?"

In many cases, the Ghostmaker doesn't just have a

problem with you—she has a problem with assistants in general. That problem, of course, would be "not realizing that they are individuals with names and personalities." Take this story, for example:

> Two weeks ago my company had a huge party for their twentieth anniversary. As the senior exec assistant, I had to do most of the planning. My boss wanted it at this fancy hotel that has a big dining room. I got everything reserved and taken care of. Then the day before the party my boss told me there was one last thing to take care of. He got out the floor plan of the dining room and asked me to make a seating chart—for the execs. Turns out he wanted all the execs at one table in a very specific arrangement (with him at the head of the table, obviously). I asked where the assistants were going to sit. He basically wanted them at this smaller table way in the back of the room, just far enough so they couldn't hear any of the execs talking. Oh, and he didn't give a shit if they had seat assignments. After all, they're just assistants, not human beings, right?
>
> —Caroline, Chicago

THE IDEA THIEF

In this coveted assistant position, you actually get to work on projects and come up with ideas. Don't get attached to any of the ideas, though, since that contract you signed means every single thing you so much as imagine while at work becomes your boss's property. Since he's a nice guy, he will give you a nice fruit basket as thanks when he gets his end-of-the-year bonus.

The Idea Thief

WHAT HE WEARS: Unassuming, generic business gear. All the better for blending in.

WHAT HE DRINKS: Whatever the person he wants to suck up to is drinking, because he learned in some business book that you should copy people you want to be like.

FAMOUS EXAMPLE: Sigourney Weaver as Katharine Parker in *Working Girl*.

HOW TO COPE: Keep copies of *everything*. And I don't mean "save e-mails on your work computer." E-mail things to your personal Gmail account, keep dated copies of every document, and make sure there are copies at work and at home.

Also, take an extra-close look at the contract before you sign it. If you can, ask a lawyer (feel free to hit up a friend in law school, somebody's relative, or anyone else in your peripheral sphere who has some legal knowledge) to take a look at your contract and clarify the part about whether the company owns your ideas and, if so, in what capacity. If you're well into the job and have already signed the contract, it still couldn't hurt to know the specifics. While you probably won't sue the company, keeping records is a good way to at least be able to prove to people at the company why you're valuable and should be promoted—right over your useless boss.

THE MICROMANAGING JACKASS

Did you put everything in alphabetical order? Well, you should have also color-coded it. You can't take lunch until he does, you're shackled to the desk all day so clients don't have to go to voice mail (especially when the second assistant is out sick), and he asks you to report on gossip among the assistants. Who was at the happy hour last night? How much did they drink? He might be reading your e-mail, but you shudder to think it, especially because you're so busy drawing a color-coded diagram of his brand-new camera because he can't be bothered to read the instructions.

The Micromanaging Jackass

WHAT HE WEARS: A double-breasted pin-striped suit, solid gold cuff links that used to belong to someone famous, and a silk tie tied in a Windsor knot.

WHAT HE DRINKS: Dirty martinis. Very, very dirty.

FAMOUS EXAMPLE: Bill Murray as Frank Cross in *Scrooged.*

HOW TO COPE: Try to predict his behavior by observing patterns. Does he always ask you to go fetch napkins right after he's made you bring in coffee? If it starts happening on a regular basis, make sure you have napkins in your back pocket. That way when he asks—don't offer, wait for him to ask—you can whip them out right then and there. The reason I tell you to wait for him to ask is that micromanaging jackasses like to demand things. If you anticipate that he'll want a napkin and hand it to him without asking, he'll come up with a new request immediately—nondairy creamer, a straw, Splenda, you name it—and you will be less likely to be able to fulfill it.

Micromanaging Jackasses often throw around their wealth in weird ways, like $400 desserts that they don't eat or solid gold letter openers. One assistant got fed up seeing her boss throw money in every direction except toward her:

> *I hate consultants. I feel like they get paid to stand around and tell people how to do their jobs differently—not better, just differently. And then they get paid a ton of money. Anyway, my boss just hired the worst consultant ever. She's a chair consultant. She gets paid money to tell people how they can sit in their chairs more comfortably. For extra, she adjusts your keyboard. WTF? My boss just can give*

*me a couple thousand bucks and I'll tell him to sit on
a cushion. I get paid next to nothing for making his
coffee just the way he likes it, but he pays some new
age idiot a ton of money to move his keyboard around?
I think I need to switch careers.*

—*Lindsay, Chicago*

THE CLICHÉ

He behaves inappropriately, soaks up company funds,
treats you like a secretary, and might even have a funny
smell. He has some pretty neolithic ideas about women
in the workplace, still thinks people power-lunch, and
leaves suspicious white residue in the bathroom. Of
course, the Cliché can also be a woman: her vision of
feminism is still stuck in the eighties, like her haircut and
much of her wardrobe. She also thinks people still power-
lunch and leaves suspicious white residue in the bathroom.

WHAT HE WEARS: The height of *Swimming with Sharks*
chic. Bonus points for shoulder pads.

WHAT HE DRINKS: Coffee before ten a.m., and brandy
the rest of the day. And when you set the mug down in
front of him, he calls you "sweetheart."

FAMOUS EXAMPLE: Dabney Coleman as Mr. Hart in *9 to 5*.

The Cliché

HOW TO COPE: If your boss is doing something that you consider to be sexual harassment, say something. Keep a journal of every incident that happens—be sure to jot down specifics. That way, when you go to HR or a higher-up, you'll have something a little more substantive than just your verbal complaint to give them.

Furthermore, don't be afraid to stand up for yourself—especially in front of other colleagues. If possible, try to leave his office door open or suggest that you two discuss the meeting you're coordinating in a more public part of the office like a conference room. Be firm and calm, and say things like "Mr. So-and-so, I appreciate your offer of theater tickets but I don't think it's appropriate to spend time together socially outside of work." Not only will you have witnesses, you'll do your part to create a better working environment by getting support from your coworkers.

Sometimes the Cliché has to take a class about tolerance or sensitivity in the office and then bumbles around, trying to be PC about his casual racism and sexism. Take this guy, for example:

> *One day I was driving my boss to yoga and he somehow brought up the fact that my last name is Irish (along with being Irish, I'm English, Czech, French, German, etc.) and he starts sort of awkwardly with "Well, so, you know. I am Jewish and you know how Jewish people like to feed people and eat a lot, do you and your family, like you know, being Irish, do they drink a lot?"*
>
> *What the fuck.*
>
> — *Laura, Philadelphia*

BUZZWORD: EXECUTIVITIS

A damaging but increasingly prevalent condition where a person, normally an executive, becomes so accustomed to having an assistant at his or her beck and call that the person is no longer able to do anything for him- or herself. In extreme cases, this can include using a telephone, having conversations with people who are not colleagues, and wiping themselves after going to the bathroom.

THE MARTYR

Nothing is ever her fault. Even when something bad happens to her as a direct result of something she did, she acts like she's sacrificing herself to save other employees. Whether the company loses a huge client or the fax machine is broken again, she just sighs, puts her hand to her head, and starts humming the opening bars of "Nobody Knows the Trouble I've Seen." She threatens to quit whenever she is "unjustly punished" or "cruelly reprimanded," but everyone knows she'd rather mope around the office to get attention than leave and have people stop listening to her.

WHAT SHE WEARS: Clothes that make her look younger (and less professional), like leggings, plastic jewelry, and headbands.

WHAT SHE DRINKS: Not alcohol, because imbibing so much as one sip of booze turns her into an even bigger spoilsport than she already is.

The Martyr

FAMOUS EXAMPLE: Mimi from *The Drew Carey Show*.

HOW TO COPE: Be blasé. If you agree with her repeated cries of "It's so hard for me," you're enabling her. If you totally blow her off, she'll go even further into martyr mode. So what to do? Take the middle path. Give her generic responses like "That's too bad." Better yet, add "I need to get back to work now." Maybe your dedication to your job will inspire her to actually get some work done.

THE OVERSHARER

Like the Frenemy, he wants to be your best friend. Unlike the Frenemy, he's not doing it so he can secretly sabotage you later. No, the Oversharer is usually needy and craving attention or companionship. Nothing is off limits: his kids, his sex life, his therapy sessions, his wife's hot flashes. He often encourages you to share your own personal stories so that he can feel like the two of you are really "connecting," but all you want to do is go home and bleach your brain until the image of him and his wife experimenting with bondage is out of your head forever.

The Oversharer

WHAT HE WEARS: Ill-fitting and/or unflattering office gear spiced up with "quirky" accessories, like a pin shaped like a golf club or a tie with music notes printed on it.

WHAT HE DRINKS: Bottomless cups of chai from a mug that has some corny inspirational word or phrase on it: think "DREAM BIG!" or "TEAM—Together Everyone Achieves More."

FAMOUS EXAMPLE: Michael Scott on *The Office*, who has absolutely no concept of boundaries—or dignity.

HOW TO COPE: If you're stuck listening to yet another one of his monologues about how he and his brother had an argument last week about politics and can you *believe* anyone thinks that way, go ahead and smile and nod—but don't stop working on what you're working on. That way, you at least have something to occupy you while you're pretending to care about his story, and Excel spreadsheets will never have seemed more interesting. Plus, he might eventually get the hint that you have other things to do besides weigh in on his inane family microdramas.

If he can't—or won't—take the hint, you might want to fire back with some oversharing of your own. He may feel totally fine sharing details of his personal life in the office, but he might weird out when you decide to share back and finally realize how inappropriate it is for a boss and an assistant to know that much about each other's personal lives. Also, you can make sure that whatever you decide to disclose is a roundabout way of telling your boss to stuff it—for example, "My girlfriend and I had a huge fight the other day. She says she's really sick of listening to me talk about work and thinks I might need to establish some boundaries."

THE BEST AND WORST CELEBRITY BOSSES

Despite living in the post–*Devil Wears Prada* world, when the horrors of celebrity assistant life became common knowledge to anybody with an Internet connection or a multiplex nearby, why do people continue to aspire to a job as a celebrity assistant? If you type "celebrity assistant" into Google, you get pages and pages of tips about how to snag one of these "coveted" positions and the contact information for staffing agencies that brag about which famous peoples' peons they count as clients. Sadly, in a celebrity-soaked culture, people dream about any profession that gets them within air-kissing distance of even the most D-list reality show contestant. Some people are willing to tolerate the abuse and nonstop caretaking that comes from working for divas because, let's face it, the perks can be pretty great: free drinks, guaranteed entry into VIP areas of exclusive clubs, comped travel to remote and exotic locations, and a possible side career selling celebrity secrets to tabloid magazines. Jake Halpern's 2007 book *Fame Junkies* analyzed people who sought careers as celebrity entourage members, particularly assistants. He conducted a study of 653 middle school students in his hometown of Rochester, New York, and gave them a list of possible professions, asking them which one they'd most like to be when they grew up. The options were: CEO of a corporation, a Navy SEAL, the president of Harvard or Yale, a United States senator, or the personal assistant to a very famous celebrity. You can guess which job won. Halpern notes:

> Of the thousands of people who work in Hollywood—agents, lawyers, stylists, publicists, business managers, and others—many gravitate toward the town's biggest stars. What is unique about celebrity personal assistants is that such proximity appears to be the only perk their profession offers. Most assistants describe the bulk of their work as drudgery—doing laundry, fetching groceries, paying bills. And unlike lawyers and agents, who rub shoulders with the stars *and* often make millions of dollars, assistants are not paid particularly well. According to a survey administered by the ACPA [Association of Celebrity Personal Assistants], celebrity personal assistants

typically make about $56,000—not much money
by Hollywood standards, especially considering
the around-the-clock obligations they have.*

However, not everyone who aspires to celebrity as-
sistantdom is just looking for a job as a hanger-on. Plenty
of wannabe actors, musicians, screenwriters, and direc-
tors work as assistants for people in the entertainment
business in hopes of making connections that will pay off
in the long run. If you're good at your job and have a decent working relationship with your boss, it is possible to
parlay your connections into a longer and more lasting
gig in the industry. I'll introduce you to some of those
successful folks in the next section.

Although you can find celebrities who don't have
personal assistants (Tim Gunn, Ellen Page, John C.
Reilly), the truth is that most celebrities have a person—or
three—who gets paid to manage their lives for them
24/7. After all, what's the point of being famous if you
can't order someone around? Allegedly, assistants are
supposed to do actual work—tasks such as managing
a celebrity's busy schedule, booking travel, and making
sure all the pages in the endorsement contract are signed.
But many celebrities treat their assistants little better
than indentured servants, making them personally hand-
engrave birthday party invites or run to the store for
Cheetos and Red Bull at two a.m.—and not sharing. For

many "famous" people who don't actually have jobs or do anything that requires assistance in the first place, having an assistant is just like having a Birkin bag or a little yappy teacup poodle. In other words, a celebrity assistant is often another accessory.

Find out who makes the list of the worst celebrity bosses, and then you can stop seething for a sec and read about some famous people who actually treat their underlings with respect. They're pretty rare, though. You know, like unicorns.

THE WORST

• NAOMI CAMPBELL: If bad celebrity bosses had a patron saint, it would be Naomi Campbell. The diva British supermodel developed a reputation for treating everyone in her employ like dirt. But then, something magical happened. Unlike any boss you've ever worked for, Naomi actually had to go to court to defend her assistant abuse. Naomi was convicted of assault (she threw a phone at a maid named Ana Scolavino when she couldn't find the pair of jeans Naomi wanted to wear on *Oprah*) and was ordered to do community service by cleaning some buildings on New York's Lower East Side. Naomi tried her hardest to make light of the situation through the only means of expression she knows about—fashion—by wearing totally expensive and inappropriate outfits for her janitorial work. She also has been spotted in a shirt that reads "NAOMI CAMPBELL HIT ME" on the front and

"AND I LOVED IT" on the back. Despite the community service and anger-management classes, Naomi Campbell appears not to have learned anything about how to treat people with respect. That's why, until she makes amends to the assistant community at large, STA is more than happy to follow her every misguided move.

• RICKI LAKE: Celebrity assistants are known for having to do some crazy tasks, from going on a four a.m. condom run to personally clipping and painting the toenails of the boss's dog. But possibly the single grossest horror story I have ever published on STA was the story about how Ricki Lake's assistant had to clean up after Lake gave birth to her son in her bathtub. Yeah, you read that right. Some poor assistant had to clean up Ricki Lake's fucking afterbirth. And what could possibly make this story worse? Well, I didn't hear it from Lake's (obviously beleaguered) assistant. I heard it from Ms. Lake herself, who told it as an "amusing" anecdote in an interview she did to publicize a documentary she made about home births called *The Business of Being Born*. Hey, Ricki? Your story isn't cute, and instead of making you look like an earth mother it made you look like a slave driver. Even if you're paying your assistant a million bucks a year, it's not enough.

Ricki's story was so gruesome that I've started using it as shorthand around the site, especially when deciding which horror stories make the cut for getting published.

"Is it as bad as cleaning up Ricki Lake's afterbirth?" is basically my way of measuring anything. So, uh, thanks for that, Ricki.

• **ANNA WINTOUR**: the bitch who launched a thousand blogs. The notorious editor of style bible *Vogue* is known for treating assistants like crap, but they put up with it in order to guarantee themselves careers in the hypercompetitive fashion world after they've paid their dues. One former assistant, Lauren Weisberger, published a thinly veiled account of her time working for Wintour in *The Devil Wears Prada*, which became first a best seller and then a hit movie starring Meryl Streep in the Wintour role. Soon, "angry ex-assistant lit" became its own subgenre, with Bridie Clark dishing on publisher Judith Regan in *Because She Can* and Rachel Pine describing what life was like working for the Weinstein brothers in *The Twins of TriBeCa*.

The real crime isn't that Anna Wintour abuses assistants—it's that she continues to get away with it. Unfortunately, as long as Wintour has a glamorous job that other people covet, she'll never have any incentive to stop torturing her underlings.

• **JOHNNY ROTTEN**: You never know what's going to push a celebrity boss over the edge. In the case of former Sex Pistols singer Johnny Rotten, aka John Lydon, it was the horror that he was in a hotel room that did not have a shared door with the room occupied by his assistant, Rambo. In his fury, Rotten attacked his other assistant—a woman named Roxane Davis—and screamed obscenities at her. She later sued him for assault and battery, since it's apparently not possible to sue someone just for being a giant douche bag.

• **ARTIE LANGE:** Best known as Howard Stern's sidekick, Artie had a personal assistant named Teddy who booked Artie's comedy gigs and ran his errands. Because this is *The Howard Stern Show* we're dealing with, Teddy of course got mocked and teased on the air. One day, though, it went too far, and Artie tried to physically attack his assistant and had to be restrained. The next day, Artie resigned from the show (although the "resignation" didn't last for long) and later entered a rehab facility to deal with heroin addiction. Needless to say, giving an evil boss drugs that make him more evil is never a good idea.

• **MARIAH CAREY:** Mariah Carey may in fact be the Queen of the Assistant Entourage. Her army of assistants doesn't just include someone to manage her schedule. Mimi's a diva, which means she needs one assistant to carry around extra hot rollers (in case her hair falls limp during a long day of shooting a music video or doing a photo spread), an assistant to carry around breast tape (in case one of her micromini dresses starts budging too far southward), and an assistant whose entire job is to hold on to Mimi's drinking straw so she doesn't smudge her lipstick while enjoying a white wine spritzer. If the economy ever hits her hard and forces her to downsize, she could probably jettison the breast tape assistant and just start wearing dresses that fit properly.

• **MIKE MYERS:** While it's not exactly shocking that some celebrities treat their assistants like crap, Mike Myers is one of those special celebrities who treats other people's assistants like crap. When he was taping an appearance on *Late Night with Conan O'Brien,* Myers was a total divo, demanding that set production assistants (who obviously have nothing else to do, like, say, make sure the show starts on time and the microphones work) fetch him some Twizzlers, raspberry seltzer, and nondairy creamer. Maybe Myers could have pulled some of that shit when he was still making really funny movies, but I'm sure anyone who had to sit through *The Love Guru* can agree that he is not important enough to send PAs scrambling around Manhattan on his behalf.

• **DAVID HASSELHOFF:** While David Hasselhoff might be entertaining in theory (makes amusing YouTube videos when drunk, has fun "don't hassle the Hoff" catchphrase), he seems to be pretty difficult in practice. The notorious D-lister also fancies himself somewhat of a ladies' man, although he probably has more success in Germany than in the States. So that Hasselhoff won't have to deal with the actual work of asking women for their phone numbers and potentially being shot down, he has an assistant who is dispatched over to any woman Hasselhoff finds appealing. The assistant then hands over a card with Hasselhoff's number on it. I'm sure that when the assistant applied for this job he wasn't aware it involved pimping. That's why you should always read the fine print, people.

• LINDSAY LOHAN: The troubled starlet got headlines all over the world when she was busted for a DUI. However, I found the story behind the DUI way more interesting than the actual arrest. It turns out that Lindsay's second assistant, Tarin, had quit that evening and called her mom to come pick her up. When Tarin and her mom drove off, a very intoxicated and angry Lindsay gave chase, and the assistant's mom called the police to tell them someone was following her. The police caught Lindsay, she almost immediately went into rehab, and the rest is history.

Even before the drama with Tarin, Lindsay got into a public fight with actress Jessica Biel when Biel "stole" Lindsay's assistant, Lindsay Ratowsky. Good celebrity assistants are pretty hard to come by, and it sounds obvious that if someone had the choice between working for a drugged-up, hotel-room-trashing star or a more laid-back one, anybody would choose the option behind door number two. Lindsay didn't think so, and yelled at Jessica during a glitzy party for *GQ* magazine.

THE BEST

• KATE MOSS: Fiona Young spent seven years working for the British model and finally quit—not because of trauma resulting from multiple stilettos being lodged in her skull, but because she was pregnant with her first child and wanted to become a full-time mom. Although Kate was reportedly heartbroken at losing her assistant, she understood Fiona's decision and threw her a huge, star-studded baby shower with tons of free stuff donated by companies Kate had connections with.

Later, Kate honored her daughter's nanny, Mary Davidson (who also happens to be the mom of Kate's best friend, actress Sadie Frost), on her birthday by "trading places" for the day. The nanny spent the day enjoying a champagne brunch and a shopping spree. Kate, presumably, looked after her own child.

• R.E.M.: Some journalists would kill for the kind of celebrity access that an assistant gets. That's not always a good thing, particularly if "access" means being on the receiving end of a cell phone to the head. But for David Belisle, who spent several years as the band R.E.M.'s personal assistant, access meant that he got some one-of-a-kind pictures of the group. Belisle, whose dream was to be a photographer, spent seven years working for R.E.M., and after he moved on he published his photos in a book, *R.E.M.: Hello.* Lead singer Michael Stipe wrote the introduction for the book and even appeared at a couple of Belisle's book signings to show support.

• **KATE BOSWORTH:** Plenty of bosses and assistants have pleasant, cordial relationships with each other, but sometimes they can become real-life friends. That's what happened with actress Kate Bosworth and Jacqui Louez, who was her assistant during the shooting of *Superman Returns*. They become such good friends during the shoot that they stayed in close touch afterward, and when Jacqui got married Kate flew to Australia to serve as a bridesmaid. In this case, not only could a celebrity and an assistant be friends, but the celebrity could even willingly take a backseat to the assistant on her special day.

• **NEIL GAIMAN:** The beloved sci-fi author often uses his personal blog to interact with his fans, talk about upcoming projects, and mention whatever he's thinking about now. Occasionally, he refers to his personal assistant, Lorraine. When people wrote in asking questions about Lorraine and what her job was like, Neil let her speak for herself by writing some posts on the blog. Turns out that the author and his assistant had quite a mutual admiration society—Lorraine, an artist and musician, relished the freedom that her job gave her (she works a set number of hours per week, and portions them out during the week depending on what else she has going on) and Neil loved how Lorraine kept his otherwise hectic life organized and sane. It's nice to see a boss/assistant relationship that's so healthy and appreciative.

• **CHELSEA HANDLER:** E! talk show host and comedian Chelsea Handler loves to include her personal assistant, Chuy "Little Nugget" Bravo, into her jokes and sketches (since he's a little person, most of these jokes have to do with his size. Who would have guessed?). However, it's clear that her jokes are only in good fun, because when it comes to Chuy's career, Chelsea is always willing to help him out. Evidence? Chuy nabbed a book deal with help from his boss, who has published several essay collections.

• **BRUCE SPRINGSTEEN:** The Boss's longtime friend and personal assistant, Terry Magovern, died in 2007 after battling cancer. While even the least compassionate boss probably would have come to the funeral or sent money to the family, Bruce went one step further, writing a song in his late assistant's honor. That tune, "Terry's Song," was premiered at a Springsteen concert in April 2008 on what would have been Terry's sixty-seventh birthday and appeared as a hidden track on the album "Magic."

• **SARAH JESSICA PARKER:** Though her alter ego, Carrie Bradshaw, thanked her assistant by buying her an expensive purse, actress Sarah Jessica Parker has a reputation for rewarding her assistant in a more useful way. In his book, *The Perfect Scent, New York Times* perfume critic Chandler Burr details the process behind making Sarah Jessica's perfume, Lovely. Burr met with Sarah Jessica's assistant, Melinda Relyea, and reported that Melinda was happy and fulfilled by her job and by how respectfully she was treated. Melinda even snagged an associate producer credit on the *Sex and the City* movie.

• **STONE PHILLIPS:** When news anchor Stone Phillips was let go from his longtime job at NBC because of network budget cuts, his assistant was able to stay on at the company. Although he could have just retreated to his summer house and waited for a book deal, he bought his assistant a new car in order to thank her for all her service over the years. It's one thing for your boss to give you a note on your birthday, but it's another for him to publicly thank you even after he's not under a work obligation to do so. Oh, and in case you were wondering, it was an Audi.

• **ANGELINA JOLIE:** Considering how much money and fame Angelina Jolie has, it's easy to imagine her being a total diva. Luckily, her assistant Holly Goline reports that Angie is a great boss. She and Goline are close friends, and the assistant is often a jolt of reality in Angelina's crazy, tabloidy life. How close are they? The two got pregnant (Jolie with twins Knox and Vivienne) around the same time and posed for tons of pictures together at

Cannes in almost-identical white flowy maternity dresses. Sources in New Orleans, where Angelina and Brad Pitt own a home, have reported seeing Angelina and Holly out enjoying a drink together.

Because of their close proximity to famous people, it's not uncommon for celebrity assistants to wind up in relationships with celebrities. Examples include Christian Bale and his wife, Sibi Blazic (former assistant to Winona Ryder, she and Christian met on the set of *Little Women*); Elisha Cuthbert and her former fiancé, Trace Ayala (assistant/best friend of Justin Timberlake); John C. Reilly and his wife, Alison Dickey (former assistant to Sean Penn, she and John met on the set of *Casualties of War*); and Alejandro Sanz and his reported wife, Raquel Pereda (who used to be *his* assistant, which caused a scandal when they got outed as a couple in the Latin media). In one of the most unusual examples, Roseanne Barr's assistant Becky got married to Bill Pentland—Roseanne's ex-husband. While she was able to do double duty for a while, ultimately Becky decided to leave her assistant gig for good in order to remain on good terms with Roseanne, whom she still considers a close friend.

Now, not every great boss happens to be a celebrity, and not every great boss can afford to buy his or her assistant an Audi as a "thank you for playing" parting gift. Here are a couple examples of regular people who showed that they were awesome bosses:

• **LEONARD ABESS JR.:** When he retired, Miami-based boss Abess sold the majority stake in his company for $60 million. While he could have just used the hefty chunk of change to buy himself a beach house or a private plane, Abess doled out bonuses to every single employee of the company—including several who had recently retired or left the company. The bonuses were based not on title but on length of service, and in some cases totaled more than $100,000.

• **BARRY DIXON:** A lawyer based in Syracuse, New York, Dixon came to rely heavily on his assistant, Pat Fowler. Even though thanking her once in a while could have been enough to show his appreciation, Dixon went one step further and penned an article in a local trade publication where he sang Fowler's praises. "I have subscriptions to many industry publications, but they hit my desk a few weeks late, dog-eared and covered with Pat's highlighter marks," he wrote. "Believe me, she can hold her own in any room filled with advisers."

• **IAN "MOLLY" MELDRUM:** Meldrum, a music producer in Australia, couldn't bear the thought of losing his assistant when she had a baby. Instead of forcing his assistant, Yael Cohn, to choose between work and family, he redesigned his studio to be more baby-friendly so that Cohn could bring her son to work with her and he let Cohn set her own schedule.

• **CHRIS JERNIGAN:** Some bosses show their appreciation for their assistants with gifts or bonuses. Chris Jernigan, the director of North Carolina–based Southmountain Children and Family Services, went five steps further than that. When his assistant, Lisa White, needed a kidney transplant, Jernigan had himself tested—and was a match. You read that right—*a boss gave his assistant a kidney*. After the successful surgery, the two of them appeared on *Good Morning America*. When Jernigan was asked about his motivation, he responded, "This was just one more thing that I was able to do to help out a good friend and an employee."

• **ANONYMOUS EXECUTIVE:** When Hollywood mega-agencies William Morris and Endeavor merged in 2009, plenty of employees—from assistants on up—lost their jobs in a purge. *Variety* magazine reported on the firings, and they even quoted one unnamed executive, who said that her top immediate priority was helping her recently-let-go assistant find a new job. And they say no one in Hollywood has a heart.

THREE

The Rest of the Office

If you don't like your job you don't strike,
you just go in every day and do it really half-assed.
That's the American way.

—HOMER SIMPSON

Why talk about bosses before talking about coworkers? Well, the truth is, most assistants spend the majority of their time at work in direct or indirect contact with their bosses. Your boss is the person who sets your priorities and gives you the tasks that keep you running around the office or glued to your computer all day. You get so much face time with your boss—or phone time, or yelling-across-the-office time—that he or she is the main focus of your life at work. Plus, your relationship with your boss is the one that's the most fractious and perilous—if you don't get along with a coworker, it's annoying, but if you don't get along with your boss, you may wind up fired. That said, there's still an important cast of characters occupying the rest of the office. The more you know about them and the more success you have working with them, the better your work life will be. Even if your boss is a giant well of crazy, having the rest of your officemates on your side will do wonders for your morale and your well-being.

First off, here are the people you need to be friends with, no questions asked—or, at the very least, be on "first name and always say hi in the hallway" basis with:

• The Receptionist—because you want to make sure that when an important package arrives for you or your boss, you'll get it immediately. Also, when your boss's client is coming in from out of town for a special meeting or his kids have the day off from school and want to come see where Daddy works, the receptionist can make sure that they get special treatment.

• The Janitor/Cleaning Crew—because their jobs are pretty damn thankless, and they have to clean up after your boss, who has a habit of leaving half-used containers of nondairy creamer and cigarette butts all over her office. Besides, you never know when you're going to spill coffee all over the front lobby and ask them to come clean it up with whatever magical stuff they have so you don't get in trouble.

• Whoever Is in Charge of Your Getting Paid—for obvious reasons.

• Whoever Is in Charge of Getting Clients Paid—like I said.

• Anybody Who Orders Food for the Office—particularly if he or she honors requests.

• Somebody in HR—if you go to complain about your boss's indiscretions, it's really helpful if someone in the department is already sympathetic to your cause.

But, of course, the coworkers you really want to have your back are your fellow assistants. They're the ones who will show you the ropes, give you all the dirt on which coworkers are "secretly" hooking up, and cover for you when you screw up. Unfortunately, though, not all assistants are tuned in to this sense of camaraderie. Sometimes they're power-trippy or backstabby, and while it's sad for the assistants as a class, it's not rare to have one of these people in your office. So see how many of the following types you have lurking around the office, and start making some friends.

THE VETERAN: This assistant may be the "senior assistant" or may have just been around the longest. Whichever, she is incredibly important to the office and to you. The senior assistant may be officially or unofficially in charge of training new assistants, but even if it's not her job she often ends up helping, supporting, and mentoring the new hires. Think of Joan Holloway from *Mad Men*—

she knows every single thing there is to know about the office, from work habits to personal lives, and is willing to share her vast knowledge as long as you are competent and don't get in her way. Make this person your new best friend, pronto. She probably has a lot to teach you, not only about how to do your job but about the complex power relations and personal conflicts that underlie all actions taken in the office. Unfortunately, in some cases the veteran assistant lets her imaginary power go to her head and ends up being a mini-tyrant of the office fiefdom, like in this story:

> So my very first ever real-world, rent-paying, oh-my-god HOW-much-student-loan-debt-do-I-have job was as an exec admin assistant to the VP of Nameless Department (VPoND). Now VPoND was queen of her nameless department and everyone bowed to her will. She naturally had her pet people, most of whom were on the "special" side of the intelligence scale—but they were mostly related to her, so go figure. About three weeks after I started, Alpha Pet informed me it was Boss's Day:

> ALPHA PET: "*Today is Boss's Day. What did you get VPoND?*"
> ME: "*...*"
> ALPHA PET: "*Don't tell me you forgot it was Boss's Day! You didn't even get her a card??*"

ME: *"There's seriously such a thing as Boss's Day? You're not pulling my leg?"*

ALPHA PET: *"..."*

ME: *"Okay. The answer is 'no' then. My bad."*

Alpha Pet immediately runs to tattle and fifteen minutes later I was called in to VPoND's office for a lecture on the importance of maintaining office morale. VPoND then tells me not to expect anything for Administrative Assistant's Day to which I respond: "There's an Administrative Assistant's Day too? No way!"

Oh to be so young and foolish again ... but I think my revealing of utter ignorance saved me from immediate firing. I still didn't get VPoND anything on the following Boss's Day. My bad.

—*Sarah, Charleston*

THE PROM COMMITTEE CO-CHAIR: Whenever there is an office party or event, you can be sure that this perky, sociable coworker is organizing it. She remembers people's birthdays and passes a card around the office for everyone to sign and gets everybody to chip in for a flower arrangement when a coworker has a baby. Though her Mary Sunshine attitude may sometimes get on your nerves, she's essentially a nice person who wants to make other people feel good about themselves. Befriend her and not only are you more likely to get a box of candy on your birthday, she might let you weigh in on the catering for the next office party—or even sneak some booze in.

DEBBIE DOWNER: Possibly the exact opposite of the Prom Committee Co-chair, this employee is happy only when she's making other people miserable. If you are excited because you just got a raise, she'll mention that you're still making less than she is, or that you have student loans to pay off but she doesn't. DD knows how to take the fun out of any situation. You're constantly figuring out how not to invite her to happy hour, but she always finds out and tags along anyway. Sometimes the best way to deflect DD is to try to play her game better than she does—at the very least, maybe you'll bum her out so much she stops inviting herself along.

RECOMMENDED ASSISTANT READING

Need something to read on the subway or during your down time? Here are some of my favorite workplace books (don't worry, I mean actual literature, not *Who Moved My Cheese?* or *What Color Is Your Parachute?*). They might inspire you to try a new career or, at the very least, give you a new perspective on the hellhole you currently work in.

Fear and Trembling by Amelie Nothomb:

A young Belgian woman goes to work in Japan and gradually works her way down from assistant to bathroom cleaner. Simultaneously funny, depressing, and full of probing questions about why we let our jobs define who we are.

Then We Came to the End by Joshua Ferris:

Set in a Chicago ad agency, Ferris's National Book Award–nominated novel follows a variety of employees through the ordinary monotony of their jobs and shows how they react when one embittered employee freaks out and goes too far.

Free Food for Millionaires by Min Jin Lee:

A middle-class girl finishes college and moves to New York City, thinking she'll easily find a good job. All of her rich Ivy League friends use their many connections to get cushy jobs, but she works in a hat shop. Great writing and a relatable heroine, but it might bum you out a bit if it hits too close to home.

Personal Days by Ed Park:

One by one, the employees of an unnamed New York company are getting laid off. The group of coworkers who form the book's heart are alternately pathetic and poetic, and underneath the narrative there's a fun element of a whodunit.

e by Matt Beaumont:

It's a workplace novel told entirely in e-mails.
It could be a gimmick, but Beaumont's dead-on
wit and characterization make it eminently
readable. Everything's there, from the feuding
assistants to the cokehead boss to the frenemies
and the workplace hookup. Way to redefine
"epistolary" for the twenty-first century, dude.
His followup, *e Squared*, is also hilarious and
updates the formula by including texts and
instant messages.

I Was Told There'd Be Cake by Sloane Crosley:

In this collection of essays, the one that deals
with the workplace is "The Ursula Cookie,"
which is a must-read. Crosley describes her
experience as a miserable assistant and makes
you totally wince and feel her pain when she
makes a cookie shaped like her boss's head in
an attempt to get her boss to like her.

Post Office by Charles Bukowski:

If you like your books about working to be dark,
well, then, this is the book for you. An alcoholic,
notorious womanizer realizes that his poetry
won't pay the bills and gets a proper job working,
as you might have guessed, in the post office.

Do Not Deny Me by Jean Thompson:

Thompson writes well-structured short stories

about ordinary people living ordinary lives that always have more just underneath the surface. The standout from this collection is "Mr. Rat," about a corporate drone at a soul-sucking company who finally realizes that he has a special gift that will help him survive at the office.

THE ASPIRING EBERT: He thinks everybody wants to know what he thinks. He may be an accountant or a public relations guy, but in his secret life, he's a movie—or music, or TV, or sports, or whatever—critic. No day can go by without this coworker talking really loudly about how *24* just isn't that good this season and if *he* were the director, he would have done so many things differently. Every time his pontificating makes you want to construct a noose out of shoelaces and packing tape, try to remember that his obsession with cinema verité or rockabilly music is probably just a way to make his very boring life seem interesting, and you should have some pity for him. That, and you can just put on your headphones and drown him out if need be.

THE IMAGINARY MOGUL: Even though he's just an assistant like the rest of you, this coworker loves to present himself as if he's a big power player. He shows up in suits and ties, even though it's a casual office, because he has taken the saying "dress for the job you want, not the job you have" a bit too much to heart. He wants people to address him as "Mr." instead of by his first name and is always jetting off to some networking thing or political meeting or charity benefit after work. He may be kind of full of himself, but sometimes being around him can pull you out of a rut and remind you about what you'd actually like to be doing with your life. And, when you do get that motivation, maybe you can tag along to his Future Executives Happy Hour and meet some new—and potentially helpful—contacts.

THE GRANOLA: We should all do our part to take care of our planet—that goes without saying. But some people take their environmental concerns *way* too far and become downright sanctimonious about it. This greenie is the kind of employee who follows people around making sure they throw their soda cans in the proper recycling bin, has an e-mail signature reading "Please consider the environment before printing this e-mail," as if anyone actually prints e-mails anymore, and sends around annoying all-staff missives about how we should all use our desk lamps less because our lamps increase global warming or something. If the Granola is in a position of authority, he talks a good game about how everything should be "organic" and "green," but usually can't provide practical ways to act on his buzzwords. Often, the Granola goes way deep into "overzealous" territory, with amusing results, like in this case:

> *My company keeps saying they want us to be more green, I don't even think they know what green is. It came up in our annual planning meeting but no one could give examples of how we'd be more green, I think they just hear the word on TV a lot and want to sound cool so they say it. Well, to my shock they finally had an idea for how to make the office more green. They hung up signs all over the copy room above each of the machines that was like BE THOUGHTFUL ABOUT HOW MUCH PAPER YOU USE—BE GREEN!*
>
> *Thanks for "being thoughtful" before you printed out all those signs on paper, jackasses.*
>
> —*Julia, New York City*

THE TECHNOPHOBE: The stereotype is supposed to be that bosses are clods when it comes to using the Internet and so they hire assistants who are super tech-savvy, right? Well, leave it to this assistant to be the one all the other assistants have to bail out. It's as if he's radioactive: a fax machine that was working perfectly begins spitting paper all over the room as soon as he touches the "start" button, an espresso machine suddenly makes wheezing noises when he goes to place his cup in it. In the end, it's worth the extra time it might take for you to make the guy some extra copies because it saves you an hour rejiggering the scanner later.

THE PART-TIME PHARMACIST: There is someone in every office who keeps a handy stash of contraband, whether it's cigarettes, alcohol, or Advil. Unless you're straight-edge, this person is your new favorite person in the entire office.

Just be careful about your relationship with the Office Drunk or Office Stoner. They're good to have around, but don't let them get totally out of hand or disruptive at the office or implicate you when they get busted. They could end up like this person:

> I'll never forget this woman at my company's Christmas party a couple years ago. OMG she was a hoot. She got drunk at the bar before the party even started and then made her rounds of the room, insulted the man who was going to be her boss, and just went on and on. That was the last party we had where the company provided entertainment, a band, dancing, etc., and a free hotel room for the night. After that all they did was take us out for dinner.
>
> The last we saw of her was her husband tossing her over his shoulder to carry her out and that Monday we came to work and her shoe was sitting on her desk waiting for her. We didn't know why the shoe was there but learned afterward that the woman she

reported to directly had placed it there and when the
girl showed up for work she fired her. She didn't even
get to work there for one solid day.

—*Rina, New York City*

BUZZWORD: SURVIVOR'S GUILT

When half your company has been laid off, but you're still employed, you feel guilty for simply having a job. It feels even worse if any of the fired people were your friends or people you were friendly with at the office. You obsess over why you're still standing but they let go people with more qualifications, more experience, and more people at home to support than you.

That said, you quickly get over your guilt because the company has assigned you all of the work that was previously being done by two people who were higher on the ladder than you, but you're not getting a raise, promotion, or even title change.

THE MASSEUSE: In my first office, there was an older, slightly skeevy dude who was always greeting all the assistants (mostly young women) with huge bear hugs. It seemed like he was just a friendly guy, but there was

something off-putting about him. Sure enough, once
he felt comfortable enough to hug you every day, he
came around the office offering free backrubs to help us
"de-stress." With this guy, you're better off never accept-
ing the hug in the first place—yeah, it may make you
seem mean, but just lie and say you have issues with personal space or are a germophobe. If he thinks you're too
mean for a hug, he'll probably also not want to skeeve on
you, which is always a plus.

The one exception to this rule? In an episode of the
show *How I Met Your Mother*, Barney (Neil Patrick Har-
ris) told Marshall (Jason Segel) that he needed to find a
"niche" in the office to protect himself from getting laid
off. One of the options bandied about? "Creepy Backrub
Guy." If Marshall was proffering free backrubs, I would
definitely accept one, sexual harassment policy or not.

**THE GUY WHO'S DOING THIS UNTIL HE GETS "DISCOV-
ERED":** Hey, there's nothing wrong with having ambitions beyond being an assistant—after all, who doesn't
want to get promoted to a job where they don't have to
make copies for three hours a day? However, this assistant has no desire to move up in the industry—he'll tell
anyone who asks (or who doesn't) that he's just doing this
gig until his acting/singing/modeling/competitive Ping-
Pong career takes off. This also means that you're constantly getting e-mails inviting you to go see his band or
one-man show or whatever. It may be annoying, but it

couldn't hurt to befriend this guy for two reasons: (a.) he might know some cool people or invite you to a premiere/ art opening/concert that you'd actually like to attend, and (b.) if he ever *does* become famous someday, you'll be able to say you knew him when. Also, if he's writing a novel based loosely on the goings-on at your office, you want to make sure you're one of the good characters.

BUZZWORD:
THE SATURDAY BLUES

Normally, workers love Saturday. There are parties to go to, beers to drink, and beds to sleep late in. But when you're looking for a new job, Saturday is a really depressing day. Since everyone else has the day off, it means your job search has to halt for forty-eight hours. When you're desperate to find a gig (or a new one that's better than the one you're currently toiling away at), that means all day Saturday you focus on how your phone isn't ringing with calls from recruiters, nobody is updating the job boards you obsessively refresh all day, and that résumé you e-mailed in time for the weekend will be on the bottom of the pile by Monday. Time to go out, have a good time, and try not to think about your fruitless job search—if you can afford it.

THE HYPOCHONDRIAC: She used up all her sick days a mere two months into the job—if it's not a cold, it's the flu or even chicken pox (even though she told everyone she had it last year). Plus, she's convinced she has carpal tunnel syndrome, so she makes the office manager buy her a fancy ergonomic keyboard. Not to mention that because of her repeated sicknesses, the Hypochondriac is always either way behind on learning how to do something and needs you to get her up to speed or hopes that you'll cover all her work for her so she can go home early—and, even though you're swamped and going to have to stay late, she does her best to work the guilt. Of course, she'll never return the favor.

THE UNDERMINER: No matter what awesome thing you accomplished today, this employee will find a stealthy way to make you feel like shit or to cut you down. For example, you're in the break room telling everyone about this awesome Marc Jacobs coat you got for 80 percent off at a sample sale, and the Underminer manages to deflate the whole room by mentioning that while the coat is great, it's a pity how that checked pattern makes your small chest look even smaller. Sometimes, you have to out-undermine the Underminer, but normally it's best to freeze him out, especially if you try to call him out on his underminerness and he insists he's just "helping." If the Underminer were on a reality show, his catchphrase would either be "I'm not here to make friends" or "People can't handle me sometimes because I just tell it like it is." Unlike Debbie Downer, who seems genuinely to be a miserable person who doesn't realize how depressing she is, the Underminer is well aware of what he's doing—he's a stealthy asshole who uses his cutting "humor" to make you feel like shit and inflate his own ego in the process.

THE RICH KID: She's working at this job only for fun, as she never misses a chance to remind you. While she may do the same work as you, she doesn't have to deal with the day-to-day stress of paying bills, since Mommy and Daddy pay for her apartment, her car, and her unlimited shopping budget. While the rest of you try to look professional with your vintage-shop finds, she waltzes in with a new designer outfit for every day of the week. Plus, her boss is really nice to her because her dad is well-connected and he doesn't want to offend any potential investors. If the Rich Kid is nice and otherwise cool despite your massive envy, remember that making friends with her could mean she invites you to the family cabin in the Catskills for Memorial Day weekend.

Here's one example of a really awful Rich Kid coworker:

I was working at a nonprofit in D.C. for a summer before grad school, and there was this one coworker I totally hated. He was a spoiled rich boy and the son of a governor. Everyone in the office got signed to a minimum two-year contract but spoiled rich boy (SRB) was starting law school later that year, so he got a special nine-month contract, which was bullshit. But we all knew they were just using him for his insider D.C. connections anyway.

SRB's lameness didn't end with his special contract. He was constantly on the phone—wasting taxpayers' time and money by not doing his job—with his Ivy law school, claiming he needed more financial aid and invoking his dad's name to try and squeeze more money out. (To their credit, they didn't budge.) To top it off, he quit at the six-month mark because he was bored working and could spend the summer in Europe. Obviously, I hated him.

—Natalie, Washington, D.C.

THE BRIDE-IN-TRAINING: While the rest of the assistants are hustling for a promotion and a raise, this girl barely seems to care. Why? She's old-fashioned and plans to work only until she can get married and start focusing on having kids. She may not even be engaged—or in a relationship at all—but hey, you're not going to judge her for her life choices. In fact, she's kind of doing you a favor by being one less person you have to compete against for that promotion.

BUZZWORD: THE MINIVENT

Sometimes you just can't hold it in another second—you're furious about something happening at work, and you really just want to throw things and scream. But since you're too responsible to do that, sometimes the best way to cope is to grab a sympathetic coworker, go outside for a couple of minutes to get air (or go buy your favorite junk food from the deli across the street), and quickly rant about whatever it is that put you in a bad mood. It may not be a full-out therapy session, but even a couple of minutes of venting will help you get your emotions out of your system before you have to run back upstairs and finish making three hundred place cards for the reception your boss is hosting tomorrow.

While you may not have to become lifelong best friends with everyone in the office, you do need to learn how to be civil to everyone and get your work done as best you can without causing problems or creating enemies. Here are some tips for figuring out how to avoid coworkers who drive you crazy and make the best relationships you can with the ones you genuinely see as friends.

. . .

Don't bone anyone you work with. Yeah, it seems like the easiest way to meet people when you spend eighty hours a week at your office, but I can't reiterate enough how bad an idea it is to hook up with a colleague. If it's a higher-up or a boss, then you're jeopardizing both your careers by getting together. If it's someone on the same level as you, you run the risk of your relationship getting in the way of your work. It seems so tempting to hook up with that cute guy who chats with you while you're waiting to get coffee in the morning, and it's easy to trick yourself into thinking that you know each other really, really well, when in truth you've only ever talked about how much your boss sucks, what funny stuff happened during the company retreat, and if you think *Saturday Night Live* is any good this season. If your crush on your coworker just won't abate, at least try to spend some time together outside the office and figure out what he is like as a person without the safe and familiar context of the office. If you really want to pursue a relationship, the best advice I can give you is for one or both of you to start combing the job boards and look for another gig. Maybe that's harsh, but it's for your own sanity. Remember the first week of college, how you hooked up with that really hot guy who lived down the hall from you in your dorm, and then he never called you again and you got a mini-wave of embarrassment every single time you passed him in the hall on the way to the laundry room? Well, screwing your coworker is like that, but doubled, because you have the realities of company policy, ethics, HR, and sheer awkwardness on top of that. Watching too many episodes of *Grey's Anatomy* may convince you that it's normal to sleep with people you work with, but you are not a television character. You are a person who runs the risk of a broken heart, being fired, or both, if you're not careful about your extracurricular activities with your coworkers.

Even if you think you can be clever and hide your affair and compartmentalize your life, you can't. The thing is, the single best way to pass the time at work isn't working—it's gossiping. And what better for people to gossip about than the likelihood of two of their coworkers sneaking out together for extralong "lunch breaks?" No matter what you do, people will know—or at least suspect—that you and your coworker are getting it on. At a company where I once worked, two employees who were playing coy about whether they were an item came in at the same time every day and then left at the same time every night, even though they lived on opposite sides of town. Sure enough, one night the office gossip was on the subway home and saw the suspected couple kissing in the car ahead of hers. They were completely busted, and from that point on nobody in the office took them—or any of their work—seriously. He ended up quitting a few weeks later, and they're still together. The moral of that story?

Date or work together. But don't attempt both at once. It's sort of like trying to Rollerblade and eat a burrito at the same time. You will get hurt. And it will be messy.

Come up with fun ways to pass the time. My coworkers and I found all kinds of amusing ways to make the days go by more quickly. For example, the hilarious game Buzzword Bingo was a big hit: just take a regular Bingo board, but instead of numbers fill the squares with different catchphrases or buzzwords that your bosses love to use, from "think outside the box" to "synergy." Then, hand the sheets out to coworkers just before you all go into a big meeting with the CEO, and come up with a subtle yet recognizable way for the person who gets Bingo first to let everybody know. You can also come up with funny, non-obvious nicknames for people in the office you don't like, make up elaborate stories about what various coworkers do when they're not at the office (Parcheesi tournaments, *Buffy the Vampire Slayer* conventions, etc.), send one another funny clips and videos you find online, start a March Madness pool, observe random holidays like Talk Like a Pirate Day (September 19) or National Ice Cream Day (third Sunday in July), or look up menus for every restaurant in a three-mile radius of your office and plan an all-assistant lunch for the following week. I also suggest finding some stuff specific to your office that would be funny—for example, is there a coffee mug that everyone in the office claims belongs to them? Hide it in a new place every week and see how long it takes someone to find it. Just make sure your pranks are mild enough not to disrupt anyone's actual work, since it's bad assistant karma to get someone else in trouble for something you did.

Organize a Hangover Patrol. Everybody has those days when they trudge into the office glassy-eyed and head-achey. So, as a group, make sure that you have hangover-beating essentials like Gatorade, ibuprofen, and ginger ale stashed in the office at all times. When somebody reports a major tequila-related stomachache, take turns bringing him water, checking on him, and covering his phone if he needs to go puke. Remember the Golden Rule of Office Politics: Do unto other assistants as you would have them do unto you.

BUZZWORD: WORKER'S FIRING

A citizen's arrest is when a regular person sees a crime being committed and is able to catch the person who did it—like a mugger, shoplifter, or vandal—and hold on to them until an actual cop arrives to make a proper arrest. Well, I think a similar system should be instituted in offices. If there's a coworker whose ineptitude repeatedly wrecks or sabotages projects the other assistants are working on, but he somehow manages to escape the scrutiny of anyone who has the authority to fire him, the workers should be allowed to hold this person down, confiscate his annoying-ass laser pointer, and wait for a higher-up to appear and can him.

Start a tradition. At the Evil Empire, all the bosses had a big meeting on Wednesday afternoons, and they usually used it as an excuse to go to some ridiculously fancy restaurant and run up a giant tab. Since that meant they were out of the office boozing it up for about three hours, the assistants spent that time ordering in lunch and hanging out in one of the empty conference rooms. Each week we'd get a different kind of food and vow to spend an hour talking about TV, our sex lives, our families, people's stories about the vacation they just returned from—basically, anything but work. (That said, exceptions could be made for snarking on someone's boss, particularly if there was someone who could do a spot-on impression of her.) Although we didn't leave the office because we were too paranoid to be away from our phones and computers, we were still able to do something together as a group that didn't involve putting together a presentation.

Other offices I've worked in or that my friends have worked in have had book clubs/swaps, guacamole-making contests, and scheduled once-a-week happy hours. Let these activities come organically—if you're the only one who loves Victorian novels, don't try to force other people into a reading group, but if several assistants have mentioned their interest in learning more about wine, it might be worth attending a wine-tasting party or class as a group.

Don't freak if you can't include everyone. While I lucked out at the Evil Empire and most of the assistants were also single women in my age range, not every office will be so uniform in the assistant class. If people with spouses and children have no interest in getting a group rate and going to a baseball game together one night because they need to go home and be with their families, don't try to guilt them into something because "we're all doing it!" Accept that people are at different places in their lives, and not everyone wants to become besties with their co-workers. Don't take it personally, and always leave the door open for people who might want to participate once in a while but don't want to make a bigger commitment.

Have face-to-face conversations. There are two really good reasons for doing your interactions with coworkers in person. First, it forces you to get up from your desk once in a while and walk over to a friend's desk—even if it's twenty feet away, you're giving yourself a break from staring at that computer screen, and your poor over-strained eyeballs need a chance to rest. Second, and more important, I always recommend that if a conversation is in any way personal, embarrassing, or something you wouldn't want your boss to read, it's smart to have it off-line. Why? Well, odds are good that your company saves all the files on your computer, which include every instant message conversation you've ever had and every blog you've ever visited. The company, sadly, is well within their rights to do so—so maybe when you want to tell your coworker about how you think your boss is a grade-A asshole, you should verbalize it instead of putting it in an IM. Ashley and I learned this lesson the hard way when we got a talking-to from the office manager about not being on IM so much. Luckily, we were talking more about what movie to see that weekend than saying hurt-ful or damaging things about our bosses, but that warning could have very easily been an outright firing. In other words—don't leave evidence.

Set some online boundaries. You and your coworkers are all on Facebook, Twitter, LinkedIn, and other social networks, so it seems natural that you should all be friends online, right? The biggest social faux pas you can make is refusing to accept the friend request of someone you see every day, so you should go ahead and befriend your colleagues online—especially if they're the ones reaching out to you. However, that digital friendship comes with stipulations. If you are genuinely real-world-outside-the-office friends with a coworker and are 100 percent sure you can trust them, go ahead and be full-on Facebook buddies. But for people you're cool with in the office and yet don't consider real-life pals (or if your boss discovers Facebook!), consider altering your privacy settings so that they don't have access to certain information of yours. You might even think about having two Facebook accounts—one for professional contacts and one for personal contacts. That way, you can network online with people in your field and can leverage your Web connections, but you can also post college photos or updates about your relationship without worrying about how you'll be perceived. Another good reason to have a BFFs-only Facebook account: you can use it to bitch about your job or the people you hate at work, with less chance of it getting back to the colleague in question. Because I had only one Facebook profile and was friends with a lot of people I worked with at a former job, I came up with a code name for my boss and made sure that only my inner circle understood the significance of the name. That way, if I posted something about "Mrs. Frizzle" in my status update, my nearest and dearest knew immediately I was having a bad day at the office, and everyone else probably figured it was a non sequitur and moved on to the next profile. And while we're on the subject . . .

That pertains to your boss, too. The problem with having such a hugely involved assistant job, where you manage every aspect of your boss's life, is that you often blur the lines between personal and professional. You may think that it's common knowledge that your boss is sensitive about his receding hairline and has Propecia mailed to the office in plain brown boxes, but it may not actually be the case. Don't get in trouble for having loose lips or for being indiscreet, especially if it's about something that doesn't matter much in the grand scheme of things. In fact, you might want to use office gossip to your advantage—not by repeating it, but by making sure your boss knows you don't take part in the chatfest. He'll appreciate your silence and realize how useful you are to have around.

BUZZWORD: HEARTACHE LEAVE

Ever wanted to take a day off from work because you were so bummed about a breakup that you (a.) ate until you got sick, (b.) drank until you got sick, or (c.) just couldn't bear the thought of being in the office? Well, one company understands. Hime & Company, a market research firm in Japan with an all-female staff, provides workers with up to three days of "heartache leave" if they're coping with a breakup. While the gesture is certainly appreciated, it would be nice if other companies in other countries started picking up on this idea. Until then, you're lucky if you can wrangle a personal day. (Incidentally, Hime—which is Japanese for "princess"—also offers their employees "shopping leave," or days off when there are good sales at the shops. I have got to get them to open a U.S. office.)

Do as much as you can for others . . . but know where to draw the line. You want the other people in your office to help you out, so you have to be willing to do the same for them. After all, assisting is all about the give-and-take, and you don't want to have an uneven proportion of take to give. If you're ever saying yes to so many projects for other people that your own work is suffering, then you need to step back and reprioritize. If you're choosing between helping two people, take into account which person has done you more solids in the past or who will owe you the bigger favor next time. Remember, while maintaining good relationships with your coworkers is a great thing to do, keeping your own ass safe is even more important.

Be cautious about cliques. It's normal to like some of your coworkers more than others—you might have more things in common with them, be closer in age, or have similar outside-of-work interests. While you're certainly not obligated to be besties with every single person you work with, keep in mind how your close office friendships might color the way people see you at the office. Remember that, no matter who you went out to dinner with last night or who you are hanging out with this weekend, from nine a.m. to five p.m. you have to be an employee first and foremost. Don't let your extracurricular friendships get in the way of making positive, useful, and beneficial decisions at the office. I'm not saying you have to be bipolar, but you do have to remember that what you do at the office every day reflects upon you. If you look like you're playing favorites, you're going to earn yourself some enemies, and you don't want to offend or alienate anyone. If you're really desperate to tell your best work friend about how that cute guy from Thursday night just called and asked if you wanted to get drinks later, try to hold on to the information until lunch. Since she's really your friend, she'll understand.

On that note, you should also be careful about handing out invites to coworkers, especially when you're asking some people to attend an event and not others. Happy hour is one thing, but if you're having a major life event—such as a wedding or baby shower—it'll be one of those huge life moments that everybody in the office knows about. Even if your best friend from the office is your best friend in real life, in order to keep things safe you might want to adopt an "all or nothing" approach to inviting coworkers—either invite *everybody*, including that annoying guy from the mailroom with the wheezy cough and the rude receptionist who everybody hates, or nobody. Depending on how large your company is, you might be able to get away with inviting all the people in your department or all the assistants—as long as you're consistent in your policy, people will have a harder time being mad. If you worry you'll hurt the feelings of some coworkers you have outside friendships with, I suggest writing them a personal note—a one-on-one conversation is ideal, but a handwritten letter is fine, too—explaining why they won't be invited to your wedding. Be honest: "I felt that it would be really inappropriate to invite some people from the office and not others. While I genuinely consider you a friend and would love to have you there, I also didn't want to cause any problems or resentments in the office. Thanks for understanding, and please let me take you out for dinner once I'm back from my honeymoon." Make sure that you notify your friend/coworker before invitations are sent out—it's one thing to know ahead of time you're not invited, but it's another thing to wait around checking the mail every day for your invite only to then find out you're not invited.

If you decide to go the "invite everybody" route, you're taking a bit of a gamble. Normally, it's only your actual work friends who bother to show up in the first place, since most people want to be invited but don't actually want to go. If you're having a destination wedding, the office loser probably isn't willing to pony up airfare just to have plans for the weekend. And you never know who will give you a present—this could be your boss's quick and dirty way of trying to make it look like he's a good person. Send a nice thank-you note, but don't be fooled.

Figure out what you do better than everyone else. You may have spent so much time figuring out all your co-workers that you haven't ever stepped back and figured out what kind of an employee you are. Pay attention to what other people say about you and your work—have you noticed that you're the first person everyone comes to about, say, what venue to choose for an event? Do you get asked to double-check others' expense report calculations because you never make a mistake in your math? Are you the coworker others rely on to be a sounding board when they've had a rough day? If you're having trouble getting perspective on what you're bringing to the company, ask a trusted coworker friend what you're "known" for in the office. You'll probably be surprised to find out what assets other people see in you. When you realize how your co-workers see you, it can have several positive effects—one, it helps you on tough days to remember that you're contributing to the team and are an important part of keeping the office together every day; two, it gives you something to tell your boss the next time he starts trying to claim that you're useless; and three, it might help you realize a skill or talent you didn't even realize you had and inspire you to cultivate it further.

Furthermore—and not to be too much of a fatalist or anything, but you have to keep stuff like this in mind—having a thing you're really good at helps a lot when the company is going through layoffs and considering getting rid of people. You'll be able to confidently say, "Everyone agrees I'm the best negotiator in the group. [Boss's name] told me they never would have landed the Kellogg account if not for me." It may sound to you like you're being gross and bragging, but, sadly, most of the time execs and other higher-ups don't know you well enough to make value judgments about you or your work. So you're going to have to tell them yourself. Even if your job isn't on the line, the same information will come in handy when you're up for a promotion or asking for a raise.

Keep your personal life off your work computer. I know that when you're at work you are constantly checking, updating, and adding notes to the Outlook or Lotus calendar that drives your work life. However, keep all your personal stuff the hell off your work calendar. Never forget that your company is totally within its rights to snoop around your work calendar and your work e-mail. If you need to send a personal e-mail to a friend, use your Gmail, or, if the company blocks all outside e-mail providers, wait until you get home or call or text instead. (It's much less likely your company records and tapes all your phone conversations.) Here's one particular work-calendar-related cautionary tale:

> *I could not believe it when my company where I work (a law office) fired one of the other assistants* the day before administrative assistants' day! *But when I found out what happened, I couldn't totally blame them. See, the assistant ("Katie") had taken a lot of sick days lately, and we all assumed she was faking because they were always on Fridays, but nobody could prove that she was faking, and besides, what assistant has never lied and said they were sick when they needed a mental health day? Well, turned out the bosses were suspicious, too. They looked at her calendar and the last couple of Fridays she had blocked off the whole day and written "Go to D.C. to visit [boyfriend]." How could she be that stupid?! If you really need a calendar reminder to go visit your boyfriend, then what kind of relationship do you guys have anyway?*
>
> —*Mark, New York City*

It couldn't hurt to e-mail yourself things from your work in-box every now and again if company policy permits. If there's a work contact you've struck up a friendship with or a document you worked on that you'd like to keep around as a reference the next time you have to write something similar, go ahead and send yourself a copy. You never know when you'll be stranded away from the office and need something—or, if you quit in a huff and they have security escort you out of the building, you won't have any luck getting back into your e-mail account.

Learn the art of the fake sick day. Sometimes, you deserve a personal day off—maybe you're hungover or just exhausted from a bad night's sleep, maybe your allergies have kicked in and you feel fuzzy-headed but not necessarily sick, or maybe you're just tired of listening to your boss's shit and want to spend the day at the spa or the beach. Whatever your reason, playing hooky is an art. Here are a few things you should know so that you don't end up like "Katie" in the previous horror story:

1. **Always call.** Some people may feel that e-mail is more impersonal/easier to fake, but a well-timed phone call is always the most convincing way to fake sick. You don't have to go all Ferris Bueller and come up with some fancy way to make your voice sound strained. Just call as soon as you wake up in the morning so

your voice has that natural crackly sound to it, and for bonus points make sure you call while you know your boss isn't at his or her desk so that you can leave a message. If you e-mail, your boss might think you're well enough to work from home, and that defeats the point of faking sick.

2. **Don't be too specific.** The more convoluted your story is, the faker it sounds. Saying "I have a migraine" or "I have the flu" is plenty. If you start going into extra detail about exactly how much your head hurts or how many times you've had to blow your nose this morning, it is (a.) kind of TMI, and (b.) sounds like a lie. (Remember, you're not a seven-year-old devising a list of symptoms in order to convince Mom to let you stay home from school, you're an adult. An adult who's lying about being sick to get out of the adult obligation of working, but an adult nonetheless.) My personal favorite go-to fake disease is food poisoning. It's quick, it's random, it lasts only a day (it's hard to explain how your flu came and went so quickly), everybody has had it before and understands how gross it is, and your boss will be way too icked out to ask follow-up questions. Plus, if he does ask, you can just say you have to go barf.

3. **Stay off social networking sites.** The easiest way to get totally busted is to blog about your awesome day off

or post Facebook pictures of you from the Phish concert you went to when you said you were sick. If you
are friends with your coworkers on social networking
sites, you *will* get caught.

4. **Be choosy about your days of the week.** If you always
   call in fake-sick on Fridays in July, everyone will be
   on to you. To fly below the radar, I recommend taking
   off random midweek days that aren't close to holidays.
   Taking off the occasional beautiful spring Wednesday
   did wonders for my mental health, trust me.

5. **Don't come in the next day with a tan.** If you are stupid about your fake sick days, you will get in trouble.
   And one of the easiest ways to stand out and make
   everyone realize you were lying is to show up the
   next day with a brand-new tan, a new wardrobe, a
   different hair color, or anything else that betrays
   what you were really doing.

6. **If you're bold, try to double it.** One of my friends has
   a great tip for those of you who want to get two days
   off in a row. She recommends calling in sick and then
   coming in anyway. It's time to start channeling the
   Martyr here, or at least reread the notes from your
   freshman year Introduction to Acting class. Don't
   shower or brush your hair. Skip your morning coffee so
   your brain is nice and fuzzy. When you come in, make

sure you look like shit, and cough and sneeze all over everything for good measure. Rub your eyes a lot while looking at e-mail. Your boss will take pity on you and insist that you go home. You can be out of the office by eleven if you know what you're doing, and then when you call in sick the next day, no one will doubt you.

7. **Take a look at a calendar** and circle days you might be planning to take off. While there are obvious ones, like a concert you want to go to or a friend's wedding you're attending, you might want to look for less-obvious times to take off. One of my personal favorite days to take off is the Monday after daylight savings time starts, so that I can get my sleep patterns somewhat back to normal. A friend of mine always takes off the day after Halloween, because it's her favorite holiday and she goes overboard with drinking and eating candy and winds up with massive sugar withdrawal/hangover. I'm also a firm believer that there should be a federal law that lets everyone have their birthday (and the next day, of course) off from work, but sadly Congress does not yet agree with me on that crucial issue.

Next, you'll want to compare your calendar with the list of holidays and other times your office is closed. If you want to take off all of Christmas week but the company gives you only the twenty-fourth and twenty-fifth off, you want as much advance notice as possible so that you can allocate your personal/vacation days and plan your travel.

Keep a diary. If you have a particular recurring problem at work, or a coworker whose behavior is consistently offensive or hurtful to you, keep a regular log of what happened and when. I once worked with someone who was really rude and dismissive to every woman he worked with, but in a subtle way. His attitude would color every interaction that he and I had, and even though he wasn't an obvious "Girls are all stupid and can't make decisions" kind of sexist, he would find sneaky ways to put me down and bash my ideas. To make sure it wasn't all in my head and I wasn't exaggerating his behavior, I jotted down brief descriptions of how each scene played out. Not only were my notes useful later on when several female coworkers launched a complaint against Subtly Sexist Dude, looking back over my journal later helped me to notice patterns in his behavior that then gave me ideas on how I could handle and respond to him. The next time he bashed one of my ideas in a meeting, I was able to turn his words around on him and force him to back down from his stance. It was pretty cool.

When you lie, lie small. Even if you weren't much of a lie teller before you started your job, many offices have a way

of making the most honest people need to tell white lies
once in a while just to keep the peace or save their sanity.
For example, that lie might be "I'm doing that right now"
or "I'm on top of that issue." While the occasional white lie
is, as far as I'm concerned, totally fine (particularly if it gets
your boss off your back or gets a yappy coworker to shut up
about something), make sure your small lies don't start
multiplying themselves. For example, don't lie about having
a sick relative you constantly need to take care of (because
you never know when you'll tell some charming story about
your youth and conveniently call said relative by the wrong
name or say they were dead when they were supposed to be
alive). Or don't lie about being Jewish so that you can take
off for Rosh Hashanah and then be surprised when your
boss nails you for not fasting on Yom Kippur a week later.

Here's an example of an assistant whose white lie
helped at the time but may not have been a good idea in
the long run:

> My boss has a mini-fridge in her office where she can
> keep her lunch or her Frappuccino or whatever. One
> day she buzzed me and asked me to come into her of-
> fice. She was sitting at her desk, sniffing a container
> of milk. As soon as I walked in she stuck the milk in
> my face and said, "Does this smell sour?" I was so
> grossed out and said, "No." She was like, "I don't
> know, it's been in the fridge a long time. Here, taste
> it and tell me if it's gone bad." There was no way I

was going to do that so I said, "Sorry, I'm lactose in-
tolerant." It worked because she pulled the milk away
and tossed it in the trash.

—*Chloe, New York City*

While Chloe's lie was clever at the time and got her out of the massively gross tasting-of-potentially-spoiled-milk situation, it might not have been the awesomest lie in the long term. What happens if her boss spies her having chocolate ice cream cake at the holiday party? Let's hope that if that happens Chloe is ready to quickly cover and say she took her Lactaid that afternoon.

WHAT TO KNOW
ABOUT ADMINISTRATIVE
PROFESSIONALS' DAY

First, and most important, it exists! There really is a holiday (albeit a Hallmark one, but who cares?) just for people like you. In the land before political correctness, it was known as Secretary's Day, but even after the name change in 1992, the idea has remained the same—falling on the Wednesday of the last full week in April, it's the one day out of the year when bosses are supposed to thank the people who answer their calls, organize their schedules, and otherwise keep their lives from falling apart. Ideally, they will thank you by giving you lots of money and a day off. Ha ha ha ha.

Have you noticed how your boss remembers his anniversary or kids' birthdays only because you mark them on his calendar? Well, go ahead and make sure Admin Professionals' Day is on his calendar. If you think it seems cheap and tacky to do so—it's not. The dude cannot be counted on to even remember to put his socks on without your reminding him, and if your options are "put it on his calendar and look really obvious" or "sit around and hope he notices," then you should pick the one that might actually result in your getting recognition. You should also conference with other assistants in the office to make sure they're doing similar things—if your boss overhears another executive talking about the gift he's getting his assistant, your boss is more likely to (a.) remember the holiday exists, and (b.) get you something as well. So much of working is about making sure you're on the same level as everybody else, and your boss is probably not going to want to be left out. Even the most tone-deaf boss realizes he will look like a bad guy if he doesn't get his assistant anything—he may not care if he looks like a douche to *you*, but he doesn't want to look bad to the other big shots at the company if they see flowers on every desk but yours. If you're really concerned about your boss's total airheadedness, you could try to be a little more obvious in your approach: For example, "Hey [evil boss's name], would you mind if I took a long lunch on Wednesday? All the assistants are going out to lunch for Administrative Professionals' Day." It's worth a shot.

However, if your boss forgets or doesn't care, you don't want your enjoyment of the day to depend entirely on him or her. About a week beforehand, start flipping through the local paper and browsing around online to see what events, discounts, and specials are available in your town for Admin Professionals' Day. (While the holiday itself is that Wednesday, the whole week is Administrative Professionals' Week.) Lots of places have lunch specials or happy hour rates for assistants, plus there are almost always funny activities to be found— there's a town in Alabama that organizes an annual "Typewriter Toss" for charity, for example. Sometimes spas or nail salons offer discounts as well. You never know. Grab one of your fellow assistants and take advantage of some of the deals out there—after all, it happens only once a year, so you might as well make the best of it.

Finally, the ultimate in good assistant karma would be not only to hope for a present or five for yourself, but to ensure the happiness of other beleaguered assistants who also suffer from a lack of respect and acknowledgment. For example, you might want to have everybody sign a card for the receptionist who is an admin but doesn't have a boss and therefore might not get a gift. Or maybe bake some cupcakes and hand them out to the interns, who will probably be eternally grateful not only for the recognition but also for the midday sugar rush.

Oh, also, there's a Boss's Day. It's in October. I wouldn't stress too much about it. There's a law somewhere that says you don't have to buy presents for people who make seventeen times as much as you. I don't know where exactly that law is, but just trust me on it.

QUIZ
Do You Have a Toxic Coworker?

Not every single coworker of yours is awesome or destined to become a lifelong friend. Luckily, you're not required to become best friends with everyone you work with, but only to be civil to one another and get your work done. That said, occasionally a coworker crosses the line from merely annoying to backstabbing or hurtful. These questions will help you figure out if your least favorite coworker is harmless, just kind of a pest, or someone you need to keep an eye on.

1. When you tell your coworker that you got a raise, he responds:
    a. "That's great! I am so proud of you!"
    b. "Awesome—let's go out drinking after work to celebrate. I'll let you buy a round, since you're rich now."
    c. "Cool, I got one, too. I guess they had a good quarter."
    d. "Wow, I had no idea they rewarded mediocrity

at this company. Remind me to stop trying
so hard."

2. What's the most uncool thing your coworker has ever
    done?
    a. Accidentally forgot to CC you on an important
       e-mail.
    b. Wore way too much cologne or perfume one day
       and smelled up your whole cube.
    c. Was the only person in the office who didn't sign
       your birthday card.
    d. Told your boss that you're a lazy slacker the com-
       pany would be better off without.

3. Your coworker's parents are in from out of town and
    she's showing them around the office. How does she
    introduce you to them?
    a. "This is [your name], who works on [whatever
       you do]."
    b. "This is [your name], who is [your boss's name]'s
       assistant."
    c. "This is [your name]."
    d. Nothing, she just walks right past you.

4. Your coworker is in charge of ordering sandwiches for
    today's assistant lunch, and the only order that got
    messed up was yours—you're allergic to tomatoes but

your sandwich has tomatoes in it. When you point it out, your coworker says:

a. "I am so sorry! I haven't touched my sandwich yet, do you want to trade?"

b. "I'm sorry, but hey, nobody's perfect. Do you want to call and order another one? Just charge it to the company account."

c. "My bad. You can just pick them off, right?"

d. "Oh, you're actually allergic? I thought you were just making that up."

5. Were you invited to your coworker's birthday happy hour?

a. Yes, she invited you once via e-mail and once in person.

b. Yes, she sent a mass e-mail out to all the assistants, which included you.

c. She invited you at the last minute.

d. No, and when you asked her if she was doing anything for her birthday she changed the subject really quickly.

6. Yesterday, you sneaked out early to go to a sneak preview of a new movie. Today when you come in, your coworker says:

a. "Hey, your boss was looking for you last night. Don't worry, I told him you were running an errand for the CEO."

  b. "Is it true Brad Pitt came to the premiere? I am so
     jealous of you."
  c. "How was the movie?"
  d. "Well, if it isn't Miss I'm-Above-the-Rules."

7. The assistants are planning the company holiday party,
   and everyone has a task. What does your coworker volunteer to do?
   a. Whatever no one else volunteered for.
   b. Something he's particularly good at—like decorat-
      ing or negotiating with vendors.
   c. Anything that's easy and won't require him to put in
      more effort than he absolutely has to.
   d. Nothing, until he finally gets assigned a task by the
      office manager. That doesn't stop him from spend-
      ing the whole party complaining about how much
      everything sucks and how he could have done a
      better job, though.

MOSTLY As:
Your coworker is totally trustworthy. He or she seems like a
good person both in and out of the office, and you'd have
to be crazy or desperate not to let this person into your
workplace inner circle.

MOSTLY Bs:
This coworker seems like a pretty stand-up guy or girl.
They're definitely worth inviting along to the group happy

hour or asking for advice on difficult projects. You won't have to spend the whole time wondering if they're planning to sabotage you.

Mostly Cs:

Proceed with caution. Your coworker might be in a perma-nent bad mood because of a jerky boss or stressful home situation, and their meanness might not be directed specifi-cally at you. Still, you never know, and while you should be civil to this person, you should definitely keep your cards close to the vest when talking to him or her.

MOSTLY Ds:

It's official—we have a loser. This toxic coworker will ruin your good days and make you even more miserable on your bad ones. Stay as far away from this person as possible, and if you absolutely have to work together, make sure to keep him or her at arm's length. Whatever you do, never give in to the temptation to gossip with this person or offer too much personal information, because it *will* get used against you.

FOUR

Getting in —and out— of the Groove

"Human beings were not meant
to sit in little cubicles staring at computer screens all day,
filling out useless forms and listening to eight different
bosses drone on about mission statements."

—*Office Space*

Don't confuse liking your coworkers with liking your job, or vice versa. It's a weird quandary to be in: part of the reason I survived as long as I did at the Evil Empire was because the other assistants were cool and helpful, but I liked those coworkers so much that I didn't leave my job as soon as I should have. I thought that if I quit, those people would stop being my friends because we had nothing in common anymore. In fact, the opposite was true: leaving the Empire encouraged me to strengthen my relationship with my coworker friends. Since we no longer saw one another every day, we made an effort to keep in touch online and hang out with one another at industry events and parties. Plus, once we all went off to different companies, my well of networking contacts grew steadily. Soon, I knew people at several companies where I was thinking about applying for jobs, and then I could call up my friends and ask them for advice or referrals.

Staying at a job you hate because of a couple coworkers you like is sort of like staying in a bad relationship just because you can't bear the thought of not having plans on Saturday night. It might seem scary to lose those close coworker connections, but if you've genuinely built up friendships with each other they should be able to last outside of work.

Start a Take This Job and Shove It Fund. Virginia Woolf once wrote that if a woman wanted to be a writer (but, more specifically, independent and able to fend for herself), she needed money and a room of her own. Unless you're still shacking up with Mom and Dad, you probably have a room—or even an apartment—of your own. What you don't have much of is money. It may suck when you're already subsisting on a meager assistant's salary, but I can't overemphasize how important it is to have some money of your own set aside just in case. Get creative with your budgeting and try to set aside a certain amount of money, even if it's only fifty bucks, every month. Make a goal to brown bag your lunch once a week and put the $10 you might have spent going out into your savings account, which is now to be known as your Take This Job and Shove It Fund. The more money you have saved up, the more you can think about your job as a job and not as something you do just to earn money.

How many times have you had a shitty day at work, come home depressed or angry, and told yourself you can't quit because you don't have any other options? Having a monetary security blanket will help you get rid of those feelings of hopelessness. Do you know why mega-rich A-list Hollywood stars can choose to work only on movies that they care about? It's because they have enough money that they can't be swayed by having to work. Take Julia Roberts, for example. Now that she's married, raising kids, and has more than enough money to get her through the rest of her life comfortably, she doesn't make a dozen films a year. She does stuff she thinks is fun (like working with Clive Owen or George Clooney—yum) or personally meaningful (producing and starring in the film version of the spiritual-quest book *Eat, Pray, Love*). While you probably won't ever have as much money as Julia Roberts, you can use her as an example of somebody who is comfortable enough that she doesn't have to work with people or on projects she doesn't want to. So squirrel cash into your Take This Job and Shove It Fund, and you'll find that you're less likely to put up with crappy or unfair work situations. Plus, if you get unexpectedly fired or laid off, you won't be completely screwed financially and can thus take the time to look for a new job that you really like and that serves your career well instead of being so desperate for cash that you accept the first offer you get despite the fact that it's not your dream gig.

Shake up your routine(s). This probably sounds like a terrible idea, but hear me out: you might want to start getting up earlier. Yeah, I know, I'm not a morning person either. But once you get into a rut at your job, it's easy to divide up your entire life into "work" and "not work." Once you do that, you start getting really predictable— you eat the same thing every morning for breakfast, have the same hang up your coat/pour coffee/turn on monitor routine when you walk into the office, and watch the same TV shows when you come home from work. The more monotonous your days become, the more you slip into a lull, and when you slip into a lull it's a lot harder to recognize when you're getting into dangerous or unhealthy patterns. One easy way to shake up your routine a little bit is, yeah, waking up earlier. Think about it: if you do some stuff for yourself in the morning, then go to work, then come home and do more stuff for yourself, you have just changed your day from being divided into halves to being divided into thirds. Even though it's not a huge change, you become aware that work is a component of your life instead of your whole life. Go for a run, spend some extra time with your dog, watch morning TV, make yourself a healthy breakfast, wash some of those dishes you were too tired to do last night, read the editorial page, drop your favorite suit off at the dry cleaners—basically, do whatever makes you feel good about starting the day and has nothing to do with work. What's a smoother transition from being asleep to being awake—chatting with your roommate over cereal and OJ, or wolfing down a bagel while your boss is shouting at you about all the stuff you have to accomplish today? Exactly.

BUZZWORD: TAKE YOUR UNEMPLOYED FRIEND TO WORK DAY

Sometimes, you and your coworkers feel like you're living in a little bubble. After all, when you spend so much time at work, it's easy to forget that the rest of the world isn't concerned with your everyday dramas and petty squabbles. That's why it's a good idea to get some fresh blood in the office. If you have a friend who is unemployed, about to graduate, or between jobs, find out if she can come spend some time hanging out in the office. Clear it with your office manager—maybe you can say she's an intern for a day, or that your college

paired you up with a current student who is interested in your industry. Once you get an okay (pro-
mise to keep her away from confidential stuff; she
may even have to sign something), let your friend
"shadow" you at your job. On one level, it could be
practical: while in college, I spent a day following
around a recent grad friend who worked at the local chamber of commerce, and it not only taught
me about what a typical workplace was like, I got
to learn about my city and how it operates. If you
have a friend who's considering getting into your
industry, she'd probably love the chance to be a
fly on the wall for the day. And it's always helpful
to have an outsider's perspective on your work
situation—if someone can spend a few hours in
your office and immediately diagnose your boss as
a grade-A douche bag, then you're probably not
hallucinating.

Examine your excuses. What's noteworthy isn't just the
fact that you're not doing your work anymore or that
you've gotten sloppy—it's *why*. One way to get some insight into how you really feel about your job is to step
back and notice what kinds of excuses you give yourself
for not completing work projects. Do you tell yourself

you'll get to it on Sunday night because you just want to have a peaceful weekend before getting back into work mode? That might indicate that you need space from work or that you're having trouble compartmentalizing. Do you tell yourself that you'll do it only after your third cup of coffee? It could mean that you're bored and looking for ways to fill up your day with distractions. Get to the heart of the real reason you don't want to do your job, and it might give you some much-needed insight about what you'd rather be doing. Then you can figure out how to actually *do* what you'd rather be doing.

Make some value judgments. Even if your job sucks, there may be parts of it that you like. If you're so focused on all the stuff you hate, it might be hard for you to step back and realize new skills you've learned or interests you weren't aware you had. For example, at one assistant job I ended up having to help coordinate a party for a VP who was retiring. I'd never done anything like it before, but the assistant who normally planned parties was on maternity leave and I got stuck filling in. Well, it turned out to be really fun. I loved working with the vendors, choosing the perfect location, and organizing the menu. (Plus, it was great to have an excuse to sneak out of work for a while to attend to "important party business" like sampling all the specialty cocktails and deciding which ones to serve at the event.) When I left that job, several of the jobs I applied for were in event planning, something I never would have considered a year or two beforehand. If you're thinking about leaving your gig, it's never a bad idea to think broadly—do you *have* to stay in the industry, or are there other things you would be happier doing or other industries you think you'd be a good fit for? It's worth some consideration. For example, a friend of mine worked at a publishing company and was dead set on staying in that exact profession, working up to becoming a book editor. Later, though, she got to know more about the publishing industry and realized she was way more interested in becoming a literary agent. She'd gone into her job with a very specific idea of her career path and then realized how many more opportunities existed in her field. This might be a time for you to think more broadly and openly about your profession.

Have a purge. Even if you're not a pack rat by nature, offices tend to become piles of clutter. That's because you have a small desk or cubicle and you probably have tons of paperwork you have to keep up with, yet no place to store it. Plus, you're stuck sitting at your desk most of the day, so you also keep a small army's worth of supplies within easy grabbing distance.

I know it sounds kind of corny, but I do believe that having a cluttered workspace sometimes leads to having a cluttered mind. If you feel trapped by your job, that feeling only amplifies when you're penned in at your desk by piles of paper at every side. So, while you can't toss out actual work-related stuff, try to steal an extra hour during the week (or even a couple of spare minutes a day, while you're on the phone, or during lunch one day) organizing as best you can. Whether that means finally filing the stuff that's been accumulating on your desk since forever or just finding a place in the office where you can stash some of the old stuff you don't need anymore, clearing up your workspace will help you to clear your mind.

One other thing to be aware of isn't just how much stuff you have on your desk, it's what kind of stuff. If you have cutesy stuffed animals, or a bowl of candy, you should strongly consider ditching them. Lois P. Frankel, author of *Nice Girls Don't Get the Corner Office*, has observed that when an employee's desk has too many personal items, particularly those labeled as "feminine" (like the candy bowl), colleagues begin to see that person as a maternal figure and thus have a difficult time envisioning that person in a management or other leadership role. It's not your fault that you are getting forced into a role based on other peoples' outdated perceptions of what a man or woman in the workplace is supposed to be, but if you become aware of something like that you have the ability to change it. Try it as an experiment—eliminate as much personal stuff from your workspace as possible and see if anyone treats you differently. People base their impressions of you as a worker on your desk space as much as your clothing choices or the way you speak, so do what you can to keep your boss from using your love of pastel-colored office supplies against you.

Look back on stuff you did when you first started. Sometimes when you're feeling particularly "stuck" or "in a rut," it really helps to take a look at your past. After all, how will you know where you're going if you don't know where you've been? If you keep a blog or journal, pull it out and flip to the stuff you wrote when you first started your job. Some of it will make you laugh or groan in retrospect, but the really important thing is that you'll realize how much you've learned. It's hard to step away from the daily monotonies of your job and see the big picture. You're so consumed with everyday phone calls, meetings, documents, and the like that you aren't necessarily able to look at your career path objectively. That's why keeping even the simplest journal can be a huge help down the road. If you're writing your résumé but having trouble characterizing yourself as a worker or listing your achievements at work, the journal will provide some of that information for you.

Also, journals help you to put things in perspective. Every time you're having a crummy day at work or something doesn't go the way you planned, it might help to flash back to a time when you were way less kick-ass at your job. In my first nonassistant job, I would sometimes feel discouraged if one of my ideas wasn't popular in a meeting or a story I suggested didn't impress my boss. To get myself out of the funk, all I had to do was think about the experiences I had back at the Empire—and let me tell you, having one of my ideas be less than enthusiastically received is way less horrible than getting a stapler thrown at my head. Once I remembered how far I'd come, my day suddenly seemed a lot more sunny. Perspective can be awesome like that.

Write your mission statement. Remember how you had to write that personal statement when you applied to college? Even though it may have seemed like a huge challenge to try to describe everything important about yourself in a couple hundred words, it was a good exercise. Now, as you're trying to figure out if you want to stay in your job, quit your job, or do something totally different with your life, one way to get started is to write your mission statement. This can just be a few sentences or a paragraph in which you write about what really defines who you are and, more specifically, what you want to do with your life. Forget about things like "I want to make a lot of money" or "I want to get promoted"—boil it down to the purest essence. For example, just to dork out for a sec, here's the mission statement I wrote about myself shortly before starting STA:

The only thing I know for sure is that I want to be a writer. But what does writing mean to me? It doesn't mean just sitting in a room writing stories— I want to write things that other people care about, and that give other people help, support, purpose, and meaning. My goal is to write primarily on-line, since the Internet is accessible to people all over the world.

There's some specific stuff here (writing, the Internet) and some vague stuff (helping people). But once I wrote this paragraph it helped me to crystallize in my head exactly what I wanted to accomplish with STA and my other future projects. Your mission statement may make you realize you want to stay in your industry but switch to another part of the business where you feel more useful or inspired. It may help you to figure out which alternate career is a better match for you. Whatever it does, writing your mission statement is a great way to get to the heart of your career goals once they're separated from all the everyday bullshit of your job.

Be subtle about your job search. If you're looking for a better job in the same industry, you'll need to be very discreet. You don't want any news of your "disloyalty" getting back to your boss. Normally, a very simple "My company isn't aware that I'm exploring other options" at the beginning of a job interview is enough to let people know that they need to keep the fact that you came into their office on the down low. Plenty of people look for jobs while they're already employed elsewhere, so there's nothing to be ashamed of. In fact, already having a job when you get an offer means that you have more power to negotiate salary and other benefits, since the second company will have to "lure" you.

If there's a coworker you trust enough to tell about your job search, make it abundantly clear that you two can't discuss it while at work. If you want to go out to lunch and talk about how well your interview went while far away from the office, go ahead. Also, if you are planning to ask a coworker to be a job reference for you, ask him about it privately—and outside of the office if possible. Check with your coworker/reference and see what contact information he'd like you to provide—is his work number off limits? Should you provide his personal e-mail address instead of his office one? The idea is to help you get a new job, not to help your kind coworker lose his.

Here's a story about one Hollywood assistant who got in major trouble regarding his job search. This e-mail was sent from Agent A at Evil Hollywood Agency to Agent B at Other Evil Hollywood Agency earlier this week. Names have been changed to protect the guilty, but spelling mistakes haven't.

Hey xxxx,

One of your partners, xxxx, has offered a job to one of our youngtil 10 agents-in-training, a young man by the name of xxxx. Apparently xxxx is looking for a new assistant, mentioned it to xxxx sister who inhi works in production, who then suggested that xxxx should meet with our employee.

I am surprised that xxxx woulcalld want to raid our young trainees and offer anyone of our employees a job without discussing it with you, his partner, first. Perhaps xxxx is not aware of our friendship. He may have been at the recent xxxx, however I didn't have the opportunity to meet him. Speaking for myself, I certainly wouldn't go and offer anyone working for your agency a position without alerting you and/or discussing it with you first, whether it be an assistant or an agent. I would certainly want your blessing before I did something like that, even if your employee had approached me first about leaving your company. If your employee approached me directly, or indirectly, I would call you and let you know about it right away.

I would suggest that xxxx withdraw his offer as soon as possible, however I leave that up to you and xxxx. I hope to hear from you soon in this regard.

All the best, xxxx

Also, remember the rules about social networks and your colleagues. If you're friends with gossipy coworkers on Facebook, don't change your status update to indicate you're applying for jobs or that you have an interview this afternoon. If you're worried that your ultraprofessional outfit screams "job interview!" consider keeping a change of clothes in your car or gym bag and changing elsewhere, or at the very least wait until you're out the door to put on your tie or suit coat. The last thing you want is to get fired before you have an offer somewhere else.

Plan what you're going to say when you get asked why you're leaving. Although the temptation to say "I'm leaving because my boss is a megalomaniacal prick who makes me clip his toenails for him" is overwhelming, resist the urge to bash your current employer, particularly if you're staying in the same industry and are interviewing with people who may know your boss personally. Come up with a standard line to say (because they *always* ask this question in interviews, and you'll need to be ready). There is a way to be honest but fair. For example, try "I'm just not feeling challenged at my job anymore and really want to take on a position with more responsibility" as a nicer way of saying "I am bored as hell and need a job where I do something other than make coffee." Or there's always "I'm ready to grow, expand my horizons, and learn more about sales/media/finance/the nonprofit world/whatever." If you're planning to switch industries, that provides you an automatic response about wanting to try something new or apply the skills you've learned doing X and become really great at doing Y. Regardless, while you may be tempted to complain about your current job, remember that your new employer might wonder what kinds of shit you'll say about them if they hire you, and they'll also worry that you have a negative attitude and aren't fun to work with. Make them love you instead of hate your boss.

When I was interviewing for jobs while still working at the Evil Empire, I realized that the company had a terrible reputation within the industry. Its reputation, in fact, was *so* bad that potential employers would ask me about the hellhole. "Oh, you work for so-and-so," an interviewer would say, making his best pity face, "how *is* that?" While it was tempting to give in and spill all kinds of dirt about EE in order to unburden myself but also to form a bond with my interviewers, I had to resist. I found that by giving a nonanswer like "Oh, I never have a dull day" or "It's been a very interesting first job" was actually more noteworthy to the potential employer than if I had flat-out talked smack. They admired my discretion but also suspected that if they hired me they could pull the truth out of me eventually. I couldn't be certain whether the person interviewing me genuinely hated the Evil Empire as much as I did or was merely testing me to see if I'd have any qualms smack-talking my employer. Luckily, I didn't take the bait. When the new company eventually hired me, I did wind up telling people there horror stories about the Evil Empire—but only once I was sure that my job was secure and I felt comfortable enough to share.

Devise your exit strategy. The characters in Ed Park's excellent workplace novel *Personal Days* each have their own "layoff narrative," which is a hypothetical scenario they've imagined about what will happen when they get laid off from their jobs. You should have your own kind of narrative planned for that blessed day when you eventually leave your job. Will you tell your boss by simply leaving a resignation letter on his desk and then quietly walking away? Will you give two weeks' notice or tell your boss to screw off and use those two weeks to give yourself a much-deserved vacation? Whatever it is, it should be formed not out of your own personal revenge fantasies (as tempting as that is, believe me) but rather based on your boss's temperament and habits as well as the general attitude in the office. If the usual way people quit their jobs at your company is to tell their boss one-on-one and then make an e-mail announcement to the entire company, do that, but you can add your own personal flair to it (sending a serious e-mail to everyone at the company but a jokey one to your close friends, asking the office manager to write the note for you, etc). Or it may involve something outside the office, like having a really fun going-away party or taking a five-hour lunch on your last day. When my best friend quit the Evil Empire, she wanted the two of us to take the elevator down one last time (we worked on the fortieth floor of a huge building, so it was a long ride) and jump up and down in it. Simple, but really funny and freeing. When I left my job later, she came back to jump in the elevator with me.

WHAT IS STOCKHOLM SYNDROME?

When people are kidnapped, they sometimes begin to show affection or sympathy to their kidnappers. In some cases, they even identify with their captors to the point where they help them commit a crime or defend them after they are freed. In a way, being an assistant is kind of like being kidnapped. Your boss sometimes imprisons you in your office, making you work late nights or weekends, not letting you ever get up from your desk or go to lunch. At first, you resist: you complain to a supervisor, refuse to stay late unless you get paid overtime, or submit horror stories about your boss to STA or another assistant support blog. But, after a while, your will bends. You become compliant. And when you get depressed or have a really terrible day at the office, you find yourself thinking stuff like "My boss wouldn't yell at me so much if I was just better at my job" or "It's been six months, I don't understand what I'm doing wrong and why I'm not improving." Congratulations, you have Stockholm syndrome.

I once suffered from this deadly ailment myself. By the end of my tenure at the Evil Empire, I was sleeping only a few hours a night, had lost my appetite, and consistently passed on chances to go out with my friends. I had all the classic symptoms of depression, but instead of realizing that I was unhappy and should do something about it, I kept blaming myself and absolving my boss. I kept thinking that it was my fault for being bad at my job, for not staying late enough or coming in early enough or being able to read my boss's mind well enough. I was convinced that my boss's screaming, yelling, and generally abusive behavior was caused by my own incompetence. Finally, a friend talked me into meeting with a therapist. At first I resisted, but finally I thought it might help me get over my insomnia.

The therapist was a nice woman in a navy blue suit. I sat down on a chair in her office and started talking about my job. All of a sudden the stories started to flow—I couldn't *stop* talking about work. I went over every bad thing that my boss had ever said, every single story about going home in tears from the office, for about forty-five minutes, at which point I started crying so hard I couldn't stop. She handed me some tissues, let me catch my breath, and then said, "I don't know you very well, and I don't know your boss at all, but if I could offer you one suggestion . . . I think you should quit your job."

And, about three weeks later, I did.

Why did it take a session with a therapist for me to finally realize that my boss's bullying behavior wasn't my fault? I think, in my case, I needed an outside opinion in order to truly see the situation. The other assistants were kind and sympathetic, but I figured that assistants would be on my side no matter what. My friends and family were the same story. I needed someone who didn't know me and who could provide an unbiased, less emotional analysis. And when this professional woman with a Ph.D. told me that I needed to quit my job, I knew that she was right.

If you think you have Stockholm syndrome, or you recognize it in one of your coworkers, don't let it go unchecked. The "How Beleaguered Are You?" quiz on page 163 is one quick way to evaluate your own level of disgruntledness/beleagueredness. If you score highly, you might want to think about what you can do to save your sanity.

HOW TO NETWORK
WITHOUT BEING A TOOL

In the office, everybody talks about networking. There are parties and meetups and Tweetups and all kinds of organized events with the intention of getting people to network. But, unless you already know a good number of the people there, you end up just standing in a corner with your overpriced cocktail, not sure who to talk to and what to say. It's true that many people get their jobs through contacts, not through job ads. And if you didn't grow up in a certain town or go to college with everybody, you're going to have to play catch-up. When I moved to New York I knew exactly one person—my cousin. He introduced me around to people he knew, but I had to do a lot of work on my own to make friends and carve out my own identity. When you're new in town, it seems like a great idea to go to networking events that get advertised in the paper or included on local Web sites—but when you get there, it's awkward and you feel like everyone already knows one another. How can you possibly start to break into established social circles without coming off as desperate? Furthermore, how are you ever supposed to get a new and better job if you don't have any connections to help you out?

Here are a couple of suggestions for meeting interesting new people and not looking like a tool in the meantime.

Acknowledge the awkwardness of the situation. If you think you're the only person who is standing around constantly checking your iPhone and feeling like a loser, you're not. So go find someone else standing against a wall looking lost and say hi. To avoid looking like a weirdo, try breaking the ice by admitting you're pretty uncomfortable with the whole "organized networking" thing. For example: "Okay, I paid eight bucks to get in

here and my beer tastes like water. How about you?" Say
it in a way that's more snarky and self-deprecating than
bitter, and odds are your new friend will laugh and agree
with you. Plus, you can acknowledge that networking itself is a pretty odd construct—"Don't you hate networking events? I feel like I'm a little kid and my mom sent
me out on a play date. I mean, I want to meet other
people who work in communications, but this is just such
an awkward way to do it." Keep the emphasis on work,
but by being open and admitting the whole process is a
little weird, you'll be able to break the proverbial ice.

Don't discriminate based on the impressiveness of someone's job title or workplace. I once went to a party with a
bunch of people who worked in magazine publishing.
One particularly annoying assistant walked up to everyone in the room, asked where they worked, and if the
response wasn't a really big-deal national publication he
just walked away. By the end of the night, no one wanted
to talk to him—the people from lesser-known publications felt slighted and dissed, and the people from bigger
publications didn't like the possibility of being used for
their status. Try to be the opposite of that dude. Even if
your dream is to write for *The New Yorker* and you end up
chatting with a perfectly nice girl who works at the *East
Sixty-eighth Street Quarterly Newsletter*, don't dismiss her
immediately just because you have no interest in having

her as a contact. First of all, she might be a nice human being in her own right and somebody you'd like to be friends with, jobs notwithstanding, and second, you never know where people's careers will take them, and it's short-sighted to blow somebody off now when she might be a "somebody" down the line.

Make it a goal to remember at least one nonwork thing about every person you exchange cards with. No one wants to be reduced solely to what he does for a living—especially not assistants. At the average networking party, you end up talking to a bunch of people, but there will probably be only a handful that you have an actual meaningful/interesting conversation with. You should follow up within a few days, and when you do you'll want to have something more to say than "Hey, remember me? We met at that assistants' cocktail hour last week." You'll want them to know you remember them as a person, not just another name on a business card you accumulated during the evening. For example, something like this works without being too over the top: "Hey, it was really nice meeting you at that assistants' cocktail thing last week. Remember how you said that the VP of your com-pany has this habit of chewing on pens during impor-tant meetings? Well, my boss did that during a meeting today—*and* wound up spilling ink all over the table and the paper he was reading off of! It was so hilarious, you would have cracked up." If you can get away with it, it's okay to make some quick notes on the back of someone's card, especially if you have a faulty memory or drank one glass of champagne too many.

Don't work the room too hard. If you go from person to person, handing out your business card, chatting for two minutes, and then moving on, you might as well just be speed dating. How do you expect anyone to remember you if your encounter was so brief he barely even saw your face? There's nothing lamer than coming home with a little stack of cards and not recognizing a single name. That defeats the whole point of networking—you should be meeting interesting people and forming new relationships, not just shoving your business card into the hands of as many people as possible. Networking isn't a contest. Furthermore, people can tell when someone is overly ambitious—and what's the incentive to follow up with, hang out with, or do business with someone who's disingenuous?

Goals are good, but keep 'em vague. The best goals to make when going to a networking event are ones that relate only to you. An example of a bad goal is something like "I simply have to meet a person who works at such-and-such company and can get me into that sold-out

Japanther concert next week." There's no way to predict a crowd of people that accurately, and if your goal is that hyperspecific you're basically setting yourself up to crash and burn. A more reasonable goal? "I have to talk to at least three new people tonight." See? That one's totally doable—because it's only about you and your ability to socialize. If you're shy but trying to become more talkative around people you don't know, maybe your goal should be that you strike up a conversation with a complete stranger. If you find that you can't stop talking about work, maybe your goal should be to limit "so what do you do?" chatting and ask more questions about people's hobbies, interests, and outside lives. As much as networking is about meeting people, it's also about seeing how you act in professional workplace situations. You can learn a lot about yourself from how you handle networking events.

Bring a friend, but don't stick together all night. If you're not brave enough to hit an event alone, by all means bring a like-minded friend with you. However, keep in mind that bringing a friend to an event often means that you two will just talk to each other all night—which is cool, since you enjoy hanging out, but it means you're less likely to meet other people. It can also be intimidating for other people to approach a pair of people who already seem to be involved in a conversation—who willingly signs up to be a third wheel? If your friend starts chatting with someone at the bar, you can go up and say hi if you want to, but it might also be your chance to say hello to the person standing next to you. If the discussion fizzles quickly you can go find your friend, but you two should be willing to separate a bit during the course of the evening. Ideal situation? You each meet some nice people and end up turning into a group.

Don't get drunk. Yeah, I know it's tempting when there are all those free drinks sitting around or you're anxious and trying to calm your nerves with a couple of cocktails, but getting drunk is the last thing you want to do at a networking event. After all, would you really like the cute guy who works at the company you'd die to work at to remember you as that girl who got really wasted and fell down in the middle of the dance floor? While you shouldn't treat a networking event the same way you'd treat the office (as in: you can probably ditch your boring blazer or put on those funky earrings), you also shouldn't behave like you're out clubbing on a Saturday night. Have a drink or two to loosen you up—or accept one if a new friend offers to buy—but that's all, especially since many networking events start immediately after you leave work, meaning you might not have had time to eat. And scarfing down two canapés or a couple of stale cheese cubes does not count as dinner.

QUIZ
How Beleaguered Are You?

1. When a friendly coworker says "Good morning!" while
    you're making coffee, you reply:
    a. "Good morning!"
    b. "Hey."
    c. "Oh, hi, [name]. Do you think you could please get
       that sales chart to me at some point today? My boss
       is tired of asking for it."
    d. Nothing—you just roll your eyes.

2. What is your office addiction of choice?
    a. Coffee.
    b. Red Bull and Twizzlers.
    c. Cigarettes.
    d. Tranquilizers.

3. The office is being renovated, and they're offering
    time and a half to any employee willing to work over
    the weekend and help pack boxes. Are you in?
    a. Sure, you could use the extra cash.
    b. Maybe if some of your work friends are doing it,
       too.
    c. Okay, but you reserve the right to show up hung-
       over and complain the entire time.

    d. No way in hell, and when the HR person comes over to ask, you respond by sticking your fingers in your ears and yelling, "I CAN'T HEAR YOU!"

4. If you got fired today, how would you feel?
    a. Heartbroken. You would totally not deserve it.
    b. You'd be hurt, then mad, and then move on with your life.
    c. You'd be upset, but also secretly relieved.
    d. You would weep with joy and then take a two-week nap.

5. What is the first thing you do when you get in to the office in the morning?
    a. Check your voice mail and e-mail and get your boss's coffee ready the way she likes it.
    b. Look at the calendar and figure out the most important task for today.
    c. Check your personal e-mail and Facebook.
    d. Submit today's batch of stories to FuckMyLife .com.

6. Do you ever have dreams about work?
    a. No, you sleep like a baby and are refreshed and peaceful when you wake up.
    b. Once you had a dream where you were at work and the fire alarm went off, but it was actually your alarm going off.

    c. You have had a couple of dreams that feature your boss or a coworker, but they're not about the office, they take place in the Amazon or outer space or something.

    d. Yes, and they're called nightmares.

7.   You're at the grocery store on a Sunday morning when you see your boss walk in. What do you do?

    a. Walk over from the produce aisle and say hi.

    b. Wave or smile, but only if he notices you first.

    c. Hide behind the cereal rack, hoping he doesn't see you.

    d. Run screaming out of the store, abandoning all your groceries.

8.   When a friend applies for a job at your company and asks you for a recommendation, you say:

    a. "Sure, I'd be happy to. Wouldn't it be fun to work together?"

    b. "I don't know how much an assistant's opinion matters, but of course I'll write you one."

    c. "Okay, but if you end up with one of the sucky bosses don't say I didn't warn you."

    d. "Are you insane?"

MOSTLY As:

You are still as bright and shiny as a new penny. Every day at work is full of moonbeams and puppies. Your friends are

jealous of you. Like the title characters in the John Mellen-
camp song "Jack & Diane," hold on to sixteen as long as
you can. Because change will come around *real* soon.

MOSTLY Bs:
You're mildly disgruntled, but most of the time have a good
attitude. If you can put up with the occasional crazy day at
the office or a weirdo client every once in a while, chances
are you'll do well at your job and be able to maintain your
sanity as well. However, if the crazy days and weirdo clients
become more frequent, you need to watch out.

MOSTLY Cs:
You are in a pretty deep funk. This is a dangerous state to
be in, because you're not flat-out miserable, you're probably just lethargic and bored. This means you're likely to be
in a rut and lose sight of your goals and ambitions. Perhaps
it's time to shake things up—you don't have to quit, but
maybe it's time to switch departments, take on some new
or different projects, or start some extracurricular activities
that make you feel more alert in general.

MOSTLY Ds:
You need to quit yesterday. And, following that, immediately enter therapy. You've definitely crossed the line between "my job isn't always awesome" and "my job has

made my life completely not worth living." Once you've reached that point of no return, nothing you do at your job—even if it's an amazing promotion—can help. You're better off cutting your losses and trying to find a gig that doesn't make you so stressed your hair falls out.

—————————————————————

FIVE

Going into the Light

The brain is a wonderful organ.
It starts working when you get up in the morning,
and doesn't stop until you get to the office.

—ROBERT FROST

So, all this time that you've been an assistant, you've been "paying your dues" and "getting your foot in the door," and now you've started to wonder how long one has to pay dues anyway and exactly how many years of your life you're supposed to spend picking up someone's dry cleaning before you get the chance to show off what you can do. The truth is, there's no magic formula. Some people start as assistants but because of layoffs or somebody quitting or a sudden job opening get promoted almost immediately. Some people have to toil away for a couple years before they can finally move up into a better position. While there isn't a perfect way to have a career, here are some tips you can use to help you figure out whether you should stay or go.

. . .

Observe your coworkers and other people in your industry. This way, you can start to figure out an average for how long it takes someone to get promoted in your field. If the last four or five assistants at your company got promoted after at least two years of being assistants, then prepare yourself to be an assistant for about two years before you start hinting to your boss that you'd like some more responsibility. In addition to noting time length, you might also want to pay attention to the circumstances surrounding their promotion. For example, did they move into an open job position? Did they spend another year in a higher up executive assistant position before getting a promotion to manager? Were they merely title changes that didn't involve many new tasks or projects (aka "promotions on paper"), or did the promoted people get new offices and start managing a team immediately? Whatever has happened at your company in the past is a good template to work from when you're starting to think about moving up. Another smart thing to do is to pay attention to what's happening at similar companies—either ask your friends about what patterns they've noticed where they work, or check out media reports or the "hirings and firings" board on a Web site that covers your industry. If you end up in your performance review stating your case for why you should be promoted, it'll be incredibly helpful to say something like "According to such-and-such Web site, the average assistant who started at a nonprofit within the last five years was promoted within two years. Therefore, I feel that a promotion at this time would be comparable with recent industry trends."

Shadow a person who has the job you want. If possible, try to spend a day or part of a day following around a person who has the job you're trying to get—either at your own company or another one. While you may have a very specific image of the job in your head, there may be aspects you didn't know about, and getting to see what this person does every day can help you not only to be more realistic about what the position entails but also to "pitch" yourself as the person with the right qualifications for said job. You'll be surprised what you find out. Does the job involve way more busywork than you thought? Are you jealous of their expense account but not the fact that they stay until eight almost every night? You may have to alter your expectations a little bit, or at least be less surprised when you land the dream gig and suddenly have to adjust to the new way of life.

Take into account external factors like the economy and the condition of your industry. As we just talked about, it's smart to know what rival companies—and your industry as a whole—are doing right now, so that you can consider that information as you plan your next career step. While it may be true that every single assistant at your company was promoted within two years, you'll need to look at context. For example, did all those promotions happen when the company was flush with profits? If they're in the red now, don't expect the same rules to apply to you. It's unfortunate that you can't time your company's success or failure to your own personal timeline, but you're not clairvoyant. What you can do, however, is make the best of the situation.

You should also look at trends that are affecting your entire industry. Even if your particular company is doing really well financially, that doesn't mean everyone else is on par with that. You need to know what's realistic to expect over the next few years.

BUZZWORD: THE "I'M OUTTA HERE" OUTFIT

Once you've quit your job and are simply whiling away your last two weeks by raiding the supply room for markers and halfheartedly training your replacement, it's time to do fun things like buck the dress code. Now's your chance to wear sleeveless shirts that show your tattoos or show up with

your swim trunks under your clothes so that everybody knows you're going to the beach immediately after work.

Decide exactly what "promotion" means for you. Not
every promotion or job change is straightforward. Don't
think that being promoted is like going from being a
freshman to a sophomore to a junior—the overwhelming
majority of jobs don't have that linear a progression. It
depends where you work—in some industries, you go
from "junior account manager" to "account manager" to
"account executive," with no derailments in between.
However, these days most people don't stay at a single
company for their entire careers. Therefore, there are a
couple of factors you have to consider when you're thinking about exactly what it will mean to get promoted out
of your assistant job. Here are a couple questions you
should ask yourself:

• If I had the choice between getting a new job title or
getting paid more, which one would I pick?

• Do I want to stay at my current company, just in a
higher position, or would I be okay with switching to another company in the same field?

- If I dislike the industry I'm working in, would I be willing to accept a demotion or lateral move in order to switch into an industry I would find more interesting or fulfilling?

- Am I frustrated with my assistant job because of my boss, or because of the kinds of tasks I'm doing every day? Would I be happy doing an assistant job for a person I liked better and was more compatible with, or am I simply tired of being an assistant in general?

- Will getting a new job solve all of my workplace-related problems, or are there larger issues that I would still need to work through and resolve?

- If my main concern is earning more money, what is the minimum amount I'd like to make at a new job? If I get an offer for a new job I like but the money isn't enough, will I accept it or look for something else?

Answering these questions honestly—and I mean *really* honestly, not just pretending you're on a job interview and saying the "right" thing—will become a huge help as you figure out what you want your next step to be. This is different from when you were looking for your first job and just applying for every single position on Craigslist you were remotely qualified for. Now that you already have your first job, you need to be more discerning and shrewd about your second job. After all, you are starting to build your career, and each job that you take is an important step in determining its shape. What's the most important to you—money, prestige, responsibility, title, positive working environment? If you need to, make a list, in order, of what things you'd most like from your next job, and then once you get an offer you can weigh it against your list. Not every job is going to line up perfectly with the items on your "dream gig" list, but it should help you to decide what is ultimately the best fit for you. Paying your dues makes sense only if they pay back in a good way.

If you've been in a rut, get out of it. It's easy to become complacent or bored when you've been doing the same job for a couple years, especially if your day-to-day tasks don't change that much. You know how on *American Idol* everyone always remembers the performance from the person who went last, but has difficulty recalling what any other contestant sang? Well, if you're being considered for a promotion, keep in mind that the people in charge often have short memories—meaning you could have been a rock star for your entire working life, but if you've been uninspired or listless the last two months, *that's* what they're going to remember. It sucks, but it's true. So, if you've been feeling monotonous as of late, try to find some ways to change it up a little bit at the office—whether that means doing all the same work but approaching it differently, or reorganizing your schedule so that you have meetings later in the afternoon when you're more alert and likely to say something brilliant instead of early in the morning when you're only into your first cup of coffee. If you wind up not getting the promotion just yet, you'll have to find ways to make your current job more manageable. Unfortunately, this is something you have to do yourself, without your boss or anyone stepping in to help. On the plus side, you can get away with referring to yourself as "a self-starter."

If your daily routine is entrenched because of your boss's habits, company protocol, or some other factor that's way bigger than you, I suggest reorganizing your cube. I know it sounds kind of cheesy, but looking at the same view every day can get really repetitive. You don't want to move things around arbitrarily to the point where you can't find anything you need, but consider putting up different photos or clearing away some of those knick-knacks, finally throwing out all that old paperwork you don't need anymore (or at least shoving it in one of the storage rooms), or just clearing up some of the clutter and taking some Lysol to the whole place. Plus, if you've noticed your wrist always hurting or that you have a tendency to get a crick in your neck after a long day of e-mailing, you might want to take this opportunity to move your computer around or finally buy a cushion for your chair.

BUZZWORD:
GOING ASSISTANTAL

You know how there was this period where a bunch of people who worked at post offices all went kind of crazy and shot up a bunch of people, and somebody caught on to the trend and coined the term "going postal"? Well, going assistantal is pretty much the exact same thing, if you just substitute a beleaguered assistant for a disgruntled postal worker. If you suspect that you are going assistantal or are about to, it's time to call in sick, eat a bunch of ice cream, or go for a massage—whatever it takes to destress. You don't want to end up like the assistant Natavia Lowery, who got so fed up with her boss, Ramones-manager-cum-star-real-estate-agent Linda Stein, that she allegedly bludgeoned her to death with a yoga stick. The only thing worse than being an assistant is going to prison.

Consider going back to school. If you feel like you need a break from the workforce or that getting additional education or training will help you to stand out from other candidates who are competing for the same kinds of jobs you want, think about going back to school. Does every single person above a certain rank at your company have an MBA? That might mean that if you want to stay at your company, you have to get one too. Find out if the company will pay for it or subsidize your education in some way if you agree to do classes part-time instead of full-time. You might also want to consider getting a vocational or technical certificate in a specific program for your industry, whether it's nonprofit management or computer technology. Any way to give yourself an extra edge—and give your brain something to do besides worry about who you need to call back today and how many sugars your boss wants in his coffee—is a definite plus for both your job and your life.

Take a hard look at exactly what your options are, both within and without your company. You can't get promoted if there's no job to get promoted into. I once worked as an assistant editor at a Web site where most employees had been there for at least five years. While that was tremendously encouraging for me when I first got hired, because it really showed that the employees liked and cared about one another and enjoyed their work, it became problematic when I realized my odds for being promoted were minimal—if no one ever quit, there was no empty job for me to move into. Eventually, I realized that the only way to secure a better job with a higher title was to leave the company and go somewhere else. Although it was hard to leave the coworkers who had become like family to me, when I ended up at a new job that filled most of the requirements on my list (higher title, better pay, more interesting assignments, flexible schedule), I knew I had made the right call. Besides, it's not as if I moved away—my former coworkers were all around and ready to hang out with me outside of the office. We still found time to have lunch together, even though we didn't sit across from one another anymore.

Examine your boss's career trajectory. If your boss spent ten years slaving away in the mailroom before being promoted, odds are good that she thinks you should follow the same path. This doesn't necessarily mean she thinks you're too ambitious or that you haven't earned it yet—it just means that she is coming from a really different perspective. Perhaps she entered the workforce when your industry was organized differently or when the economy was in bad shape. If your boss is a woman or a minority, she may have had to deal with racism or sexism that often stood in the way of her career goals. If you want your boss to help you get promoted and/or support your aspirations, then you might want to make it very clear that while you respect the path that her particular career took, you know things are different now and have another plan in mind for yourself and would love her guidance.

. . .

If you feel comfortable doing so, schedule a proper sit-down talk with your boss. You know how when you start dating someone, after a while you always have to have that "So are we exclusive? Where is this going?" conversation? My friend Michael—who did the original Web design for STA—refers to that conversation as the State of the Union Address. The talk isn't usually the most thrilling component of any relationship, but it's necessary to make sure you both are on the same page.

If your boss isn't a conniving diva or megalomaniacal dictator, and if you two have a decent working relationship, it's worth having a frank conversation about where your career is headed and what your boss thinks you should do next—the workplace version of the State of the Union Address. You don't need to suck up to him or mindlessly flatter him, but if you have concrete and honest things to say about his work, now's the time to bring them up—"One thing that I've learned from you is the importance of not getting involved in office politics, and that's been really helpful for me." You need to make it clear to your boss why you chose to ask him for help and advice, and if you have specific things you'd like your boss to do—act as a reference, back you up when you ask for a promotion—this is the time to mention them. Asking someone for help is one thing, but giving him actual, specific ways that he would be able to help you is even better. People—especially busy people who have their own stuff to do and their own careers to worry about—often need a bit of direction. Their intentions may be good, but it couldn't hurt to be explicit about what exactly they could do to help you out.

Decide what your breaking point is. If your main priority isn't quitting but storming out and never looking back, then you'll need to know at what point you might break. It's never possible to predict how and when your boss is going to say something offensive and out of line that finally compels you to quit, but you can set some guidelines for yourself ahead of time. For example, will you walk out if your boss asks you to do something illegal? Will you finally lose it if your boss says something that offends your race, religion, sexual orientation, or gender? Sometimes you can choose something in advance and stick to your decision. Other times, you might have a quitting-related epiphany, like this assistant did:

> *I was working as a personal assistant to a magazine editor. The man had no understanding of boundaries. He would even have me do things like tell his girl-friend he was too busy to talk to her because he thought that his power turned her on. One day he called me while I was on the way to work and told me to come to his apartment instead of the office. He*

claimed it was an "emergency." I showed up at his apartment. There he was in his PJs. The "emergency"? He couldn't find his glasses. Apparently he was totally blind without them! After doing a quick scan of his bedroom, I found the glasses in a crack between his bed and dresser. This guy had been constantly promising that I'd get more interesting (read: "magazine-related") work to do, but it never panned out. I quit that very day, when I realized that if I stayed I would always be his glasses-fetcher and that he had absolutely no intention of ever letting me do real editorial work.

—Daisy, New York

BUZZWORD: POST-TRAUMATIC BITTERNESS DISORDER

In 2009, a German psychiatrist, Dr. Michael Linden, coined this term to describe how workers feel when coping with disappointment or rejection. Like the similarly named post-traumatic stress disorder, PTBD is exhibited in people who have gone through some kind of trauma. Dr. Linden described the condition as a combination of anger and helplessness—for example, if you're an assistant who just got forced into a combo job and are now working sixty-hour weeks for no additional pay, it's likely you might have a form of PTBD as you stew over the injustice but know that for bigger reasons—the economy, for example—you can't do much about it. Dr. Linden noted that "instead of dealing with the loss with the help of family and friends, they cannot let go of the feeling of being victimized. Almost immediately after the traumatic event, they become angry, pessimistic, aggressive, hopeless haters."

Think of some backup plans. Suppose your company just had a huge round of layoffs—if you were spared, you're probably so busy being grateful for still having a job that you're not even thinking about your plan to get promoted right now. Or maybe your boss has promised that you'll get promoted in six months, when someone leaves the company or a new account comes on that you'll be put in charge of. Whatever it may be, you can't pin all your hopes on something that may or may not happen in the future. So start thinking of ways that you can progress in your career that might not be as explicit or straightforward. For example, if your company has a spending freeze, you might petition for a title change in lieu of that raise they can't give you—the only thing it will cost them is some reprinted business cards. If you're taking on the work of recently laid off employees, it's absolutely worth asking for a new title, even if you have to make one up. And that new title will look good on your résumé when you apply for other jobs.

If your job is in stasis mode and you haven't had much luck finding a new one, start thinking of other ways to boost your profile and restimulate your brain. Maybe that means taking on a couple of freelance projects in order to make some new contacts or get your name out there more. Perhaps it means volunteering or doing some gratis work for a company in a different industry so that when you update your résumé you'll be able to point to a whole new range of skills. You might also consider taking a night school class, especially if it'll teach you a skill that makes you more marketable, like graphic design or html—see if you can convince your job to pay for it or split part of the fee with you. (You'll have to use your awesome negotiation talents for this one: point out what an asset you'll be with your new abilities.)

Plus, remember back in chapter one when I said you couldn't let your job define your existence? That's still true. So don't forget to keep up with your favorite extracurricular activities, whether that's amateur photography, Italian cooking classes, or coaching Little League. You never know what kind of opportunities might arise from your side projects, and in the meantime they'll do their part to help you stay sane. I have a friend who worked in marketing, and as a favor she did some marketing and promotions for her best friend's band. Her free help paid off for the band—who raised their profile and sold out a string of shows—and ended up helping her land her dream job at a PR firm that specifically worked with musicians.

BUZZWORD: OFFICE AMNESIA

When you've been away from the office for a while (this normally happens when you've been on vacation, but not always) and suddenly forget how to do your job, thus forcing you to relearn basic stuff like dialing the phone and turning on your computer. No matter how long you do the same job, there will come a point when you sit and stare at your computer screen for like five minutes until you remember how to do your job all over again.

Keep it professional. If you're friends with some of your fellow assistants, and a job comes open, it's likely that several of you will throw your hats into the ring for it. As much as it will suck if you get passed over in favor of a colleague you think is less deserving, keep your snarky remarks to yourself and be polite to your friend—after all, if she's going to end up giving you work to do, you don't want her to start off hating your guts.

Any industry or profession—whether it's communications, education, technology, fashion, or whatever—is a pretty small world. Between corporate rivalries and industry conventions, it starts to feel like everyone knows one another. The further along you get in your career, the more you'll realize it's important to have good—or at least civil—relationships with as many people in your field as possible. They're the ones who will help you get jobs, recommend you for consulting positions, introduce you to people at networking events, and the like. So even if it totally sucks and your office frenemy gets promoted over you, bitch all you want to your best friend but keep it to yourself at the office. I'm certainly not saying you have to throw said frenemy a "Congratulations!" party or anything, but it's probably a good idea if you don't act like a giant asshole about losing out on a promotion. You are allowed to be bummed about it and excuse yourself from happy hours for a while so you can go home and wallow in your misery while watching *Steel Magnolias* on a loop. (Not that I've ever done that, of course. Ahem.) But when it comes to the workplace, you should keep it neutral. Don't fake a smile if you don't feel like smiling, because a fake smile can be spotted from twenty feet away. Just don't stomp around or make snide comments.

Here's some advice from my mom: if you can't say anything nice, don't say anything at all. And if you're filled with so much rage that you can barely see straight, take that rage and channel it into your brand-new job search.

BUZZWORD: "STEVEN'S LAST NIGHT IN TOWN"

There's this Ben Folds Five song, "Steven's Last Night in Town," about this dude Steven who is moving away from wherever and has this big party to celebrate. Well, at some point during the night all this cool stuff starts happening—people buy him free drinks, everyone says nice things about how much they're going to miss him, and this one girl admits she's had a giant crush on him for, like, ever. Steven's last night in town ends up being so much fun that he decides to stick around some more and turn every night into his last night in town.

The point? Sometimes there are assistants who threaten to quit—or actually do quit—and then love the whole everyone saying good-bye/people giving you presents/boss letting up on you and not behaving like a giant douche/coworkers organizing a party for you thing so much that they convince themselves their job is actually wonderful and has been this whole time. They then reconsider quitting and thus wear out their welcome.

The moral of this story? *Don't be this assistant.* Don't dick around and threaten to quit a bunch of times without following through, because it makes you look horribly indecisive at best and like a drama queen at worst. And once you become the assistant who cried "I quit!" no one takes you very seriously again. So only bust out the Q-word when you mean it, and enjoy all the fun parts of leaving your job while still retaining some perspective.

Do your research. A lot of unhappy assistants have told me that even though they have a boss they hate and who makes them miserable, they'd rather stick with her ("at least I know how to handle her," they say, or maybe "I can predict when she's going to go psycho") than start all over again with a new boss. It's the classic devil you know vs. devil you don't know conundrum.

So how can you snap out of this Stockholm syndrome–esque mind-set? Do some recon. If you've interviewed for or been offered a job working for someone, do all the digging you can on that person. What are their professional accomplishments? Did they work their way up to where they are or get lucky through family connections? What do former colleagues have to say about them? Have any ex-assistants started blogs about how much they hate them? At the very least, tap into your network of contacts and ask around discreetly—"Do any of you know Mr. So-and-so at Company X? What's his deal?" If anyone starts getting nosy and wondering why you're so inquisitive all of a sudden, say your bosses might be collaborating on a project with him, but you can't reveal anything more about it.

Keep your perspective. Remember that a promotion isn't something you're given, it's something you earn. Yeah, I know I sounded like your mom for a second there, but hear me out. Sure, you should examine industry trends and keep notes on other promotions in your office, but there's no rule that says you *have* to get promoted. More likely, you have to weigh in all those external factors and combine them with all the work that you've done over the past however-long.

THE BEST ASSISTANT MOVIES

Stuck indoors on a rainy weekend or just looking for a way to decompress after a crazy day at work? Update your Netflix queue with some of these excellent workplace/assistant-themed movies.

9 to 5

Three secretaries take revenge against their jerky boss and strike a blow for feminists everywhere. Dolly Parton is in it. Really, this movie has everything.

Swimming with Sharks

The story of a boy who goes from optimistic assistant to cutthroat Hollywood movie mogul. You'll identify with it, until you get to the part where he ties his boss to a chair and tortures him. Then again . . . maybe you will identify with that part.

Office Space

Basically, the greatest film ever made. It has a cliché tool of a boss, a red stapler, corporate-speak, useless consultants, the phrase "no-talent assclown," and workers taking out their frustrations on a copier. Also, it is pretty much impossible to get any of the inside jokes on STA if you have not seen this movie.

Don't Tell Mom the Babysitter's Dead

Back at the height of her *Married . . . with Children* awesomeness, Christina Applegate starred as a high schooler who faked her way into a summer job as an assistant. The movie is notable not only for the way she beautifully foists her job off onto a coworker while fending off the office bitch but for the horrifyingly campy early-nineties fashion.

Secretary

Have you ever thought, "Gee, my relationship with my boss is a little masochistic?" Well, just watch this delightful S and M–themed romantic comedy/office drama and you'll feel way more normal. Or perhaps you'll recognize unhealthy patterns. Could go either way, really.

Working Girl

This movie is a modern-day fairy tale (in the sense that the 1980s are in some way "modern"), with a Cinderella from Staten Island. Plucky secretary Tess comes up with a brilliant idea, and her frenemy boss steals it and passes it off as her own, but Tess (spoiler alert!) is vindicated, winning a victory for assistants everywhere. This movie is notable for gloriously trashy hair and eye makeup as well as an almost unrecognizable skinny, be-mulleted Alec Baldwin. Seriously, it took me half the movie to figure out it was him.

Van Wilder and *Van Wilder 2: The Rise of Taj*

These movies are pretty mindless, but they're also really entertaining, the film equivalents of eating a breakfast burrito when you have a massive hangover. It's all worth it to watch Kal

Penn (before Kumar was ever a twinkle in a stoned screenwriter's eye) start out as the shy, awkward assistant to Big Man on Campus Ryan Reynolds, triumph, and then get to star in his own movie. So what if the sequel was direct-to-video?

The Devil Wears Prada

The movie that brought assistant torture to the mainstream. Meryl Streep's multilayered performance almost makes you want to root for her evil boss character over Anne Hathaway's holier-than-thou assistant. All in all, this movie will just make you wish that if you have to be a tormented peon you could at least be a tormented peon with access to free designer clothes.

All About Eve

Have you ever wondered where that "assistant pretends to be nice and sweet but is secretly plotting to sabotage her boss and then take over her life" trope comes from? Wonder no more—it's from this movie. Despite being made in 1950, this Bette Davis/Anne Baxter classic is still just as relevant and fun to watch now as it was when it came out.

Clockwatchers

Possibly the only thing worse than being an assistant is being a temp, because then you don't even get health insurance. In this movie, four temps (including Parker Posey and Lisa Kudrow) deal with temp life and count down the seconds until five p.m.

Figure out what your company is missing. Ideally, when you figure out what they're missing out on or not getting right, you'll be able to think of a way to help or to improve the system. For example, is your company doing a great job publicizing events, but totally missing the boat on sites like Twitter? If you're a Twitter junkie, turn your hobby into something that can help you get ahead at work. Talk to your boss and suggest that you be put in charge of setting up your company's Twitter account and using the site to promote events targeted to younger consumers. Be sure that when you pitch your idea, you've thought out every possible follow-up question that your boss might have: know how much the new program will cost, what the repercussions will be if you don't do a good job, and whether this new project will take too much time away from your other important tasks. This is risky—it's a great way to prove yourself and show the company what an asset you are, but if it doesn't work out as well as the company wants it to your reputation might be tarnished. Make sure that the project is something you can do well, and prepare to show facts, stats, and other data that back up your work.

Fuck up once in a while. Yeah, I know that sounds counterintuitive, but hear me out. Once upon a time, there was an assistant at the Evil Empire named Lee. Lee was a great assistant—she was punctual, organized, and had a seemingly God-given ability to put up with her boss's copious amounts of bullshit. Her boss considered Lee essential—*so* essential, in fact, that he would never dream of letting her get promoted. He came to rely on Lee so heavily that he couldn't even fathom what it would be like to have to start over with a new assistant who didn't have his credit card info, kids' birthdays, and the phone numbers for his five favorite restaurants committed to memory. If Lee had been interested in being a career assistant, this would have been the ideal job for her—her boss was willing to pay her a pretty sweet salary in order to keep her happy and productive, and they had a good working relationship despite the fact that he was a massive douche. But Lee wanted to move up in the company, and she started to grow frustrated with her job. She couldn't figure out why she kept getting excellent performance reviews and regular raises but no offers of a higher position. The problem, you see, is that our dear friend Lee was actually *too* good at her job. It's sad, but true—being "indispensable" is good when the company is laying people off and you want to survive, but it kind of sucks when you're trying to move out of your current job. It may sound weird, but you need to mess up once in a while—not on a catastrophic, career-killing level, of course—in order to remind your boss that you are not perfect. If you're such a perfect assistant that he can't function without you, you're fucked. So feel free to screw up on something small like his coffee order once in a while just to keep yourself from staying trapped in assistant land forever.

Be able to plead your case. If you followed the advice from chapter one about keeping a journal of your work accomplishments and/or regularly updating your résumé to include recent achievements, now's the time to put that information to use. When you're making the case for why you should be promoted, you'll want to have all this information at your fingertips. You'll need to be able to cite specific examples of things you did or projects you worked on in order to show that you've contributed to the company and were successful.

One great tip I've heard about how to prep for a job interview is to make a mental list of different office scenarios you've been involved in—ideally, choose two or three and make sure you know the stories backward and forward. Then, when the interviewer asks you to tell about a time you challenged yourself/had to deal with an uncooperative team member/showed initiative, you'll already have a couple of anecdotes you can pull from, thus diminishing the likelihood that your mind will go blank and you'll sit there blinking and saying "uh . . ." for a while. The scenarios you should think about beforehand should be ones that involve a couple of different levels so that they're more likely to apply to whatever topic the interviewer brings up. For example, one of my own anecdotes is about the summer I spent teaching creative writing at a summer camp—it involved leadership since, well, I was the one teaching the thing; creativity; planning ahead, because I had to map out my lessons; and flexibility, since I was working with a broad range of ages and maturity levels and had to be prepared to lead different activities for different students. Another plus of that story is that it's about business principles, but it doesn't take place at an office. It gives a small insight into what kind of a person I am aside from the information on my résumé, and interviewers have really liked listening to a story about something other than a typical office scenario.

BUZZWORD:
THE WORK NEMESIS

Everybody has one—he's the Dwight to your Jim (because you're always the better-looking one, of

course), the Aniston to your Jolie. Your work nem-
esis isn't just someone you dislike, because then
you'd be able to avoid them. No, this person is assigned to work on projects with you, always com-
petes with you for the same prizes and promotions,
and has a crush on the same UPS guy as you. If you
had ointment, they'd be a fly in it. If you had a bon-
net, they'd be the bee in it. Basically, you hate
them, and now that you're leaving your job you
never have to see their annoying, too-shiny, per-
petually dumb face ever again.

Be proud of yourself. No one wants to sound arrogant,
which is why it's often so hard for assistants—particularly
women, who are often taught not to call attention to
themselves—to brag once in a while. While I'm definitely
not telling you to act like Tyra Banks and turn every conversation into a monologue about how amazing and perfect you are, it is okay to admit when you kick ass at
something. Promotions, raises, and other work recognitions don't come while you wait around fanning yourself
and hoping somebody will notice—they come when people are bold enough to ask for what they want. In other
words—don't sit around moping and waiting for that cute
boy to call you, just pick up the phone and call *him* already.

. . .

Practice, practice, practice. If you're nervous about asking your boss for a raise or listing all the reasons you deserve to be promoted—and it's natural to be scared, since you've probably never had to do this before—do a couple of trial runs first. Practice on your own in front of the mirror, or ask a trusted friend to pretend to be your boss and ask you questions. The more you've prepped, the more comfortable and less tense you'll be when the real moment actually happens. Think back to your high school debate team—would you have ever gone to a meet without doing your research and sparring with your debate partner? That's what I thought.

BUZZWORD: "DAMN IT FEELS GOOD TO BE A GANGSTA" MOMENT

There's this scene in *Office Space* where corporate drone Peter comes in for his first day of work after getting a big and unexpected promotion. He parks in his former boss's parking space, struts into the office like he's totally hot shit, and then unscrews the knobs from the conference room doors. This all happens to the tune of "Damn It Feels Good to Be a Gangsta" by the Geto Boys. Basically, your

> DIFGTBAG (looks like "giftbag"!) Moment is a time when you're a big star at work—you got promoted, you just got praised by your boss in front of the whole company, you just put in your two weeks' notice because you landed a way better job somewhere else—and you strut in wearing a great new outfit and you *own* the joint. Life does not give you enough of these moments, honestly. So make the most of them.

Be ready for the backlash. Some bosses find out that you're quitting and immediately go into regret mode. They might have a moment of clarity and apologize for the jerky things they've done in the past, or (more likely) they're doing damage control by trying to make nice with you right before you go to work for a rival or business associate. My boss did this—he bought me ice cream, let me leave early every day, and told my replacement that I was the best assistant he'd ever had (first of all, this just flat-out wasn't true because I was a pretty mediocre assistant, and, second, it did not cancel out the eight hundred or so other days he spent telling anyone who would listen that I was disorganized and stupid). If this is how your boss behaves, you're lucky. More likely, if your boss was already a grade-A asshole, he'll just continue being one, and he'll see your departure as a personal insult or betrayal. This example of an evil boss who flips out on an assistant who's moving on to something better just reminds you what you could expect after you put in your two weeks' notice:

> I am (for the next two weeks anyways) an agent's assistant in Beverly Hills, a living version of Lloyd from Entourage—except not Asian and my personal Ari Gold isn't as nice. And I'll bet that Lloyd has health insurance.
>
> Three weeks ago he got upset because I had booked him a lunch on Good Friday, which also happened to be a half day at work. The lunch had been booked several weeks beforehand, at which point we were scheduled for a full work day.
>
> When he got to work, he called me into his office to yell at me, in the process telling me that I didn't do anything right and never had. If that were the case, I asked, why had he kept me around for the last six months? "BECAUSE THERE WAS NO ONE ELSE!" And if I were really that horrible at my job, why had one of the partners repeatedly asked my boss to let me switch desks and work for him? "BECAUSE THERE WAS NO ONE ELSE!"
>
> The next morning I accepted a new job. I put in my two weeks' notice with HR and then geared myself up to tell my boss. It actually went surprisingly

smoothly. I went into his office and let him know I got a new job, but that I'd be staying two weeks to train my replacement. He just said, "Okay, that's fine." Then I heard him say, "Good thing, because I was going to fucking fire you anyways." Typical.

Most everyone has told me that I should have just asked if he wanted me to leave then and there, but I am sure as hell not going to give him the satisfaction of the "Et tu, Brute?" moment he is so clearly craving. I'm going to stay, continue doing my best above-and-beyond-the-call-of-duty work, knowing that leaving this job smelling like roses, with the respect of the rest of the office still fully intact, is a better fuck you than telling him off. He can get as mad as he wants, but I'm out the door and smiling.

—Brett, Los Angeles

Pay attention to your company's timing. Every company has its own particular timeline that it follows regarding hirings, promotions, bonuses, and the like. For example, while it's common for companies to give out annual bonuses just before Christmas/New Year's so everybody can spend their money over the holidays, it's plausible that everyone will have to wait until January so the money won't be taxed until next year. Is there a specific time of year that everyone gets performance reviews, or are they done based on when individual employees were hired or simply when bosses have the time to do them? Do all the executives take August off to spend at their country houses? These may not seem like important details, but a big part of trying to get a raise or promotion is knowing the right time to ask. For example, if you have a really great performance review it makes sense to ask for more money or a new title immediately after, while your positive review is still fresh in your boss's mind. However, if your new gig is something that will require higher-ups to sign off on it, then make sure you get everything taken care of before they all leave for the big shareholders' meeting and forget about you. As much as it sucks to have to depend on other peoples' schedules when you're ready and raring to go, that's kind of the way business works. So do everything in your power to work around the system.

When you quit, mean it. As noted in the "Steven's Last Night in Town" item earlier in this chapter, some assistants allow themselves to get sucked back in by jobs they hate simply because their quitting process goes well or they fall prey to a boss who begs them to stay and promises life will totally change for the better. If you've thought long and hard about it, socked away money, started sending out résumés for better jobs, and are otherwise confident that you're making the right decision for you, stay true to your choice.

Have you ever broken up with somebody who was abusive or hurtful in some way? He or she probably cried and promised to change and swore that if you just stuck around everything would work out, and then you know what? It didn't work out that way. If you have a particularly bad case of Stockholm syndrome, you're especially susceptible to an evil boss who swears up and down that if you just stay in your job he'll make sure everything is different from here on out. Don't fall for it. You made your choice, and you need to stand by it. If you falter now, your boss will think you're a pushover and never take you seriously ever again (if he or she ever took you seriously to begin with, that is). Check out this story of one assistant whose experience trying to quit her job confirmed that she was definitely making the right decision:

> It took a while, but I finally got up the nerve to quit my horrible job where my boss yelled at me from the moment I walked in till the moment I left. Not only was he a prick, he was a sexist prick. When I quit, he told me that he refused to accept my resignation because I was "just being emotional, just being a girl." As the father to several daughters, one of whom was my age, he thought he was an expert on female behavior. (Maybe if he was, his daughters wouldn't call him only when they needed money or had to go to rehab.) He insisted it was my "hormones talking" and that I would soon regret leaving him. I was so horri-

fied that I couldn't even respond to his stupid, sexist comments. The next morning, I got to quit all over again. It was great, except I kept waiting for him to tell me I had PMS and should wait a week to make my decision.

—*Laurie, New York City*

BUZZWORD: MULTISLACKING

Multislacking is the same thing as multitasking, but instead of working on numerous tasks at the same time, you're working on lots of random stuff that isn't related to your job. Now that you're leaving your job, you can fill your work days with important projects like beating your record Solitaire time, obsessively refreshing Twitter, and catching up with your friends on instant messenger. Since you're doing all of these things at the same time, the casual observer (aka your boss) might be tricked into thinking you're actually doing work. Let him.

Learn gratitude. When the economy sucks or you're the only one of your college friends who has managed to find a full-time job so far, you might feel ungrateful whenever you have a bad day, complain, or think about quitting. Here's what you need to know: it is possible to simultaneously be grateful for having a job and know that you'd be happier somewhere else. Yes, you're grateful for the fact that your job enables you to pay rent and bills every month. You appreciate the contacts you've made, the friends you've met, and the skills you've learned. But you may have also realized that you're in the wrong industry, your boss is a relentless douche with no hope of redemption, or that you deserve a job that lets you use your brain and be creative once in a while. Being honest—saying "I don't think this is the right place for me" or "My boss makes me miserable" or "I want to quit"—does not automatically equal ungrateful, nor does it make you a bad person. Maturity means you can see the good in a situation even while you're trying to get out of it.

THE IMPORTANCE OF BEING MENTORED

So, your boss probably sucks. And your assistant friends are awesome, but when it comes to getting advice about how to get promoted or what your next career move should be, who can you go to? You can count on your family and friends for moral support, but if they're not in the same field as you they might not know the weird ins and outs of your particular industry. So you're in the market for a mentor.

I was lucky enough to find a mentor when I quit the Evil Empire and started a new assistant job. I worked for the editor in chief of a Web site. He was a great journalist in his own right and had left a high-paying reporting job at a magazine to take a huge risk and start his own Web site. A lot of people could have become really arrogant after starting their own successful business, but my boss managed to remain humble and laid-back. Not only did I learn a lot about journalism from him, I also learned that it is possible to be both a boss and a nice person.

Not every mentor is someone you know or work with. But when you find a great mentor, it's like having a cool older brother, a wise best friend, and an inspiring professor all in one. You'll get great advice and pointers, but you'll also know that somebody has your back. Here are a couple of ideas for how to find your very own career role model.

Interact with other higher-ups at your company, not just your boss, and see if there's anyone you have a personal connection with. A big part of finding your mentor is finding someone you like as a person. There's a reason a mentor isn't necessarily your boss—it's someone you can hang out with outside of work and who you genuinely want to talk to on the phone or go to lunch with. And, also, who wants to take career advice from someone they don't like?

. . .

Contact your university alumni association. Even if you live far from home, your college might be able to hook you up with a branch of the local alumni chapter or give you contact info for some other grads who live nearby. If they have particularly detailed information or there are a lot of alums living in your town, you might even be able to specify that you'd like to get in touch with someone who works in your industry. The shared bond of having gone to the same school will give you something to talk about and will make you feel less awkward about meeting with someone you don't know.

Check out social networking sites, particularly ones with an emphasis on mentoring. Certain career Web sites specifically focus on pairing up older and younger workers. The Web site ed2010.com is aimed at young people who want to work at magazines, and they encourage assistants to sign up for their mentorship program—after an interview process, they'll connect you with a mentor, often someone a couple years older than you and slightly higher on the career ladder instead of someone your mom's age and an executive well past his or her assistant days. There are also sites with a mission to connect women, African Americans, Hispanics, or other people from similar backgrounds. Do a Google search or ask around for recommendations.

If you attend a house of worship, check to see if your church/temple/synagogue/meetinghouse has any kind of "young leaders" or "businesspeople" meet-ups. Even if there's no organized "Christians in Marketing" kind of program, it's possible that you can meet someone in your congregation who is in the same industry as you and would be happy to give you advice.

While you may not know anyone in the new city or town you've moved to, this is the time to check with your friends and family back home to see if anyone has any connections where you live. You never know who might have an interesting contact for you. If your aunt's best friend from high school is actually working in publishing like you want to, ask your aunt to introduce you, or reach out with a professional e-mail saying something along the lines of "Dear So-and-so, My name is [whatever] and my aunt is [her name]. She still speaks fondly of you and the road trip you guys took one summer during college. I've just moved to New York and am looking for a job in publishing. I understand that you work at [name of company], and I would love to meet for coffee so I can pick your brain about the industry and get some pointers."

Never, ever flat out ask a person for a job if you don't know her. How it should work is that you do your research and dress well, you meet and are generally a great person, and then the person likes you enough to recommend you for a future gig or encourage you to apply for a position and offers to be a reference.

If there's someone whose career you really admire and want to emulate, try e-mailing him. It may seem weird and stalkery, but most people are flattered to get fan mail, especially if they're not famous. In order not to sound like a psycho, just be straightforward and perhaps a little self-deprecating: "I'm really impressed by the fact that you started your own nonprofit before you were thirty. I am an assistant at a nonprofit right now and can't imagine the work it must take to start from scratch like you did." Don't go over the top with flattery, and use specific examples. At the end, try something like "Anyhow, if it wouldn't be totally weird for you, I'd love to buy you a cup of coffee and talk about how you got started and if you have tips for somebody like me." If you're worried about sounding too much like a fanboy, just keep the e-mail short so there's no room for error. And if you think it's too forward to ask them to hang out with you or you live in different places, try asking for advice or if they have any contacts they'd be willing to share with you. You never know.

FORMER ASSISTANTS DONE GOOD

There *is* a light at the end of the tunnel—and plenty of people have found it. Every time you get in a funk and convince yourself you're doomed to remain in your entry-level job forever, read one of these stories of success and remind yourself that there are many, many roads to your dream job.

What's really interesting to notice is how many different ways "dream job" is defined by these onetime assistants. Some of them started as assistants in a given industry and just worked their way up the traditional way through pluck and determination. Others worked as celebrity assistants and leveraged their connections to help secure jobs in the entertainment industry, or banked all their money and then went off and did whatever they wanted. No matter what route they took, and whether they were assistants for one year or fifteen, these former assistants are awesome examples of people who made lemonade out of their lemony jobs. They're also majorly inspiring and helpful to think about when you're having a down day.

• MARC CHERRY: The creator and hit writer of the popular series *Desperate Housewives*, Cherry's first Hollywood

job was as the assistant to then *Designing Women* star
Dixie Carter. Cherry was a huge fan of his boss, and the
feeling was mutual. "This young kid who wanted to get
into writing had come to town back in 1989 and worked
for me. All of a sudden, he had this writing job on *Golden
Girls,*" she said in an interview. "He's so talented." Cherry
thanked his former boss years later by writing a part for
her on *Desperate Housewives.*

• **JULIE JACKSON:** Julie worked as an assistant at a horrible, mismanaged company where her bosses did things
like ask her to put film in a digital camera. So in addition
to her full-time gig, she worked on a side venture, creating hilarious and snarky cross stitch designs, which
spelled out messages like "Bite Me" and "You Suck."
Eventually, her side job turned into not just a full-time
job but a bona fide craft empire—her company is called
Subversive Cross Stitch.

• **MAX SZADEK:** A career assistant for Luther Vandross until the singer's death in 2005, Max could have
just taken the money he was given in Vandross's will
and lived a nice, quiet life somewhere. Instead, Szadek
started his own nonprofit, Divabetic, which educates African American women about diabetes and encourages
prevention techniques. Not only is Szadek a mensch for
his community service work, but he's also paying tribute
to his late boss, who was a diabetic.

• **JONATHAN LEVINE:** When Jonathan Levine graduated from film school, he landed a job as the PA for screenwriter-filmmaker Paul Schrader, whose hit films include *Taxi Driver* and *Raging Bull*. Now Levine's a successful filmmaker in his own right. The first film he wrote and directed, *The Wackness* (which was based on his own experiences growing up in 1990s New York City), starred Ben Kingsley and Mary-Kate Olsen and scored rave reviews.

• **CHERYL HINES:** The comedienne, best known for her role as Larry David's long-suffering wife on HBO's *Curb Your Enthusiasm*, got her start as director Rob Reiner's personal assistant. Unlike some of the other celebrity assistants on this list, Hines didn't get any support from her ex-boss. She said in an interview that her job mostly consisted of cleaning Reiner's house.

• **LAUREN BERGER:** Lauren's probably the first person in the world to be promoted from assistant to intern— more specifically, the former administrative assistant is now known as Intern Queen. Under this moniker, she runs a Web site that posts job ads for internships around the country and offers tips and tricks for aspiring interns who want to make the best of their experiences.

• **HARVEY WEINSTEIN:** Believe it or not, the man known for tormenting assistants from L.A. to London got his start as a PA for no less than the Beatles. In his first job, Harvey ran errands for the Fab Four—now he counts Paul McCartney as a personal friend. It's a shame Harvey didn't learn about the rule of assistant karma during his PA stint, though.

• **KARA DIOGUARDI:** The *American Idol* judge has top-notch music credentials: she's written or cowritten hit songs for artists like Kelly Clarkson, Hilary Duff, and Adam Lambert. But when she was still just a newbie trying to break into the music business, she spent five years working as the assistant to the editor of industry bible *Billboard* magazine. No wonder she's so knowledgeable about pop music.

• **SIDNEY TORRES:** After working as the personal assistant to musician Lenny Kravitz, Sidney stepped away from a life of glamour and jet-setting to take on a very different kind of project. He founded SDT Waste and Debris, a sanitation company in New Orleans that helped the post-Katrina city get clean. In addition to picking up trash and disposing of waste, Sidney even invented a special lemon-scented spray that his workers use to spray down streets after cleaning.

• **JEN PERKINS:** When Jen got a job as an executive assistant, she made a pretty decent salary. However, she realized quickly that her bosses expected her to be a drone and barely gave her any actual work to do. Unhappy with assistant life, she started designing cute, vintage-inspired jewelry as a fun side gig. Now, her side job is a full-time (and aptly named!) project, Naughty Secretary Club. The jewelry line has spawned a book, a blog, and a crafting show on the DIY Channel.

• **MICHAEL ARNDT:** When Arndt won an Academy Award for writing the screenplay for the movie *Little Miss Sunshine*, he thanked the usual people: his agent, his family, the people who financed the film, and . . . Matthew Broderick? Turns out that when Arndt was getting started in L.A., his first job was as an assistant to the *Ferris Bueller* star. Years later, even though he was long past his PA days, Arndt wanted to thank his former boss for giving him his first break.

• **ODESSA WHITMIRE:** Whitmire started out as the personal assistant to actor Ben Affleck, but she became a tabloid presence when she started dating his best friend, Matt Damon. Although the couple split after two years together, Whitmire had become close friends with Affleck's sister-in-law, actress Summer Phoenix. Along with a third friend, Ruby Canner, Whitmire and Phoenix opened a high-end vintage clothing store, Some Odd Rubies, in Los Angeles. The store was so successful that they later opened a second outpost in New York.

• JASON POLLOCK: As a kid, Jason dreamed of making movies someday. His first job in the industry was working as an assistant to *Bowling for Columbine* and *Fahrenheit 9/11* director Michael Moore. After learning the ropes, Jason went on to make and produce his first documentary, *The Youngest Candidate*, about people under twenty-five who ran for public office. The film premiered at the Traverse City Film Festival in Michigan. The festival's organizer? Why, Michael Moore, of course.

• NADINE HAOBSH: While a beauty assistant at a magazine, she started a blog about her experiences called Jolie in NYC that ended up getting her fired (or, in Internet parlance, "dooced"). However, Haobsh was unfazed—she landed steady writing gigs, a book deal, and a boatload of free products (let's be honest, that's the best part). Her novel *Confessions of a Beauty Addict* is a roman à clef about her magazine assistant days.

• FONZWORTH BENTLEY: The man who got his start carrying P. Diddy's umbrella started to steal the show when he got attention for his dapper outfits. After Bentley left his assistant gig, he wrote a style book and hosted the reality show *From G's to Gents*, which helped young men get image and fashion makeovers.

QUIZ
What's Your Quitting Style?

1. If you found out while at work that you had won the lottery, what would you do?
    a. Hold the news in until the end of the workday and then rush home and tell your family/best friend/ significant other.
    b. Immediately IM your best work friend that she needs to rush over to your desk, stat.
    c. Send a mass e-mail out to all the assistants that lunch is on you tomorrow.
    d. Scream so loudly that somebody calls security because they think you're being murdered.

2. What's your least favorite of these work tasks?
    a. Making small talk on the phone while your boss takes his sweet time getting on the line with an important client who hates waiting.
    b. Running personal errands for your boss or doing anything else that isn't explicitly listed as a job duty in the employee handbook.
    c. Doing stuff that requires multiple layers of protocol and dealing with lots of people, like collecting signatures for a contract or organizing a meeting with half the company.

   d. Anything that involves boring busywork—filing, typing, scanning, you name it.

3. Do you gossip a lot at the office?
   a. No way—you try to stay as far away from the drama and conflict as possible.
   b. If there's something really juicy you definitely don't want to be the last one to know, but you also don't actively seek out dirt on your colleagues.
   c. Sure, especially if it involves someone you don't like or who treats you badly.
   d. Well, yeah, how else are you supposed to pass the time?

4. Who do you vent to about your work frustrations?
   a. No one, really—you don't want anything you've said in the heat of the moment to get back to your boss, so your complaints end up in a journal where they're safe.
   b. A close friend or your boyfriend/girlfriend. You tell each other everything, good and bad, and that includes stuff about your jobs.
   c. Your friends and family—that way, if they come to a work event they'll know which people not to talk to and who to avoid after everybody starts doing shots.
   d. Anybody who will listen. Nobody should suffer alone.

5. How many of your high school friends do you still keep in touch with?

   a. Lots of them! It seems like people who knew you back when you had a bad haircut and wore too much eyeshadow are truer than friends you've made as an adult.

   b. A few of them you still count as very good friends, but there are also a lot of acquaintances you send Christmas cards to or see when you're in town for the weekend.

   c. You wouldn't say you've stayed in close touch with anyone, but you're friends with a lot of them on Facebook so that you can keep up with one another's major life events.

   d. High school? Seriously? That was like a million years ago. You've moved on to bigger and better things.

6. What contact information did you give the job recruiter you're working with?

   a. Only your cell or home phone number, because you don't want any evidence of your job search to be noticeable or traceable at work.

   b. Your Gmail address—you might check your personal e-mail on your work computer once in a while, but otherwise it can wait until you get home.

   c. Your cell phone number. You keep the phone on while you're at the office. It's on vibrate, but if you recognize the number you can pick it up.

d. Your work number—you don't care if he calls you at the office. You get personal calls all the time there anyway, so no one will notice.

7. Have you ever fantasized about murdering your boss?
   a. No, that's something only a crazy person would do.
   b. You had a dream about it once, but you can't control what shows up in your dreams, right? You also had a dream once that you were riding a flying unicorn, and you don't even like horses.
   c. Maybe once or twice, when he's screaming at you about something that's totally not your fault and you need a visualization technique.
   d. Pretty much every day. Sometimes you write the fantasies out and send the most amusing ones to your friends in a mass e-mail.

8. Do you have a nickname for your company?
   a. Does calling it "work" or "the office" count? Because otherwise, no.
   b. Yeah, it's a variation or pun on its actual name, like "Turd-le Industries" instead of "Turtle Industries." And it existed way before you ever started working there; you just find it funny and say it sometimes.
   c. No, but you roll your eyes a lot whenever you mention the company outside of the office. Tone is everything.

   d. It changes all the time. One week it's Hell, one week
      it's Village of the Damned. You have to stay creative,
      you know?

MOSTLY As:

You want to go out like a lamb. Maybe you're afraid of burning bridges, or your boss has you so scared that you'd rather do anything but be the object of his ire. As far as you're concerned, the important part is quitting, not how you do it.

MOSTLY Bs:

You want to do it the most traditional—and professional—way possible. If you're leaving a job that you really hate and that has made your life a hell on earth, the last thing you want to do is sabotage yourself during your last two weeks. This is probably the safest route to take—it's not fun or glamorous, but you have to remember that you owe your boss courtesy and nothing else. As long as you follow protocol to the letter, you can't be guilt-tripped about staying on an extra week to train the new person. I mean, they might try to guilt-trip you anyway, but you're well within your rights to tell them to back off.

MOSTLY Cs:

You want your boss to be the last one to know. Perhaps you hate her guts, or you worry that as soon as you say you're quitting she'll fly into a hysterical panic and throw something pointy at your head. Regardless, no matter how you feel about your boss, you owe her the information. You don't have to give lots of details about why you're leaving or where you're going, but if your boss finds out she was the last one to know, or gets the news from someone else before you've told her, she will (rightfully) be pissed. And that's not going to make your lameducking week very fun.

MOSTLY Ds:

You want to exit with a bang. In fact, if it were possible to quit your job via a radio announcement or a banner behind a hot air balloon, you'd probably do it. While this bridge-burning sounds really tempting, you should probably dial it down a couple of notches. Even if you're moving to Paraguay to be in the Peace Corps and will never see any of these people again, it won't kill you to hold in a little bit of that glee. The best revenge is living well—so go do that.

SIX

The Story of Wayne: An Assistant Parable

So now that you've gotten promoted, found a better job, or decided to fuck it all and finally spend three months traveling around Australia, the bottom line is that you're not an assistant anymore. In fact—horror of horrors—you may even *have* an intern or assistant of your own to manage. Here's a quick pop quiz: Now that you have an intern, how should you treat him or her?

a. You should be as much of a jerk to him as your boss was to you. After all, you're in charge now and it's about time you got to enjoy the benefits of it. And it's therapeutic to get out all your anger and frustration on someone else.

b. You should be as nice to her as possible. She is learning, and you need to teach her and correct her mistakes and not coddle her, but it's possible to do that without simultaneously being a tremendous asshole.

If you answered a, you need to go back and read this whole book over again, because you obviously haven't learned anything. If you answered b, then congratulations—you are breaking the cycle of assistant abuse because you are mature enough to realize it's possible for people to pay their dues and learn about an industry without wanting to kill themselves. You also have showed that you're a caring person who remembers how hard you had it at the beginning of your career and you want to make sure other people don't have to go through the same torment that you did.

Many people who had nightmarish assistant experiences and don't want anyone else to have to suffer the same way make excellent bosses, because they're understanding and compassionate. However, it is possible to go too far in the other direction, and working for a wishy-washy boss can almost be as bad as working for one who throws stiletto heels at you. The first time I was a "boss," this was exactly my problem.

At a former assistant job, the other three assistants and I were given a summer intern to manage. The intern, whom we'll call Wayne, had just graduated from college and was eager to get a job and start making some headway in the industry (in this case, Web journalism). He was polite, punctual, and willing to work hard. However, he still needed a lot of help. I recognized some of myself in Wayne—he had the same difficulty adjusting from college to job that I had had. He'd been a straight-A student in college, but was having some trouble translating that into being a good employee—for example, he had lots of great ideas that he wanted to share in our daily editorial meeting, but he was unaware of our office's unwritten rule that only the top editors shared ideas in the meeting and the assistants didn't pitch in unless they were specifically asked for their opinions. Even though he had good things to contribute, it took him a while to catch on to the fact that it was considered a bit gauche for assistants—and especially an intern!—to share ideas, particularly if they contradicted something one of the senior editors had said. And why did it take him so long to figure this out? Well, probably because none of the assistants told him.

For all four of us, it was the first time we had ever worked closely with an intern, and most of us had no idea how to be leaders or how to assign work to someone else—after all, we were the ones who got work assigned to us. Wayne was available and willing to do any work we wanted him to, but none of us ended up giving him many projects.

I eventually figured out why I was such a terrible "boss" for Wayne. For one thing, because I had never managed anyone before, it was difficult for me to figure out the right way to assign work to someone. I didn't feel right just marching up to him and telling him to do something, so I ended up doing all his work myself simply to avoid the weirdness of asking him or of giving him a project but stammering out some kind of a "Do you think you could, uh, maybe, work on this . . . this thing? Like, if you have time? Um, okay, cool, whatever." The second problem—which definitely contributed to the first—is that I had major issues with the boss-assistant relationship in the first place. I was still suffering from a toxic case of Workplace PTSD from my first nightmare assistant job and, even though I'd moved on to something better and more gratifying, I still had problems with the traditional workplace structure. Somewhere in my brain I believed that if I never had the opportunity to become any kind of boss, then I could never be a bad one. In addition, I think I was intimidated by the idea of asking Wayne—a guy, specifically one who was a head taller than me—to do something. I'd been raised to believe that women were supposed to be polite and make other people feel comfortable, and it was hard for me to ask anyone to help me with anything. Combine that with the fact that the person who was supposed to be helping me was a dude, and you have a recipe for complete failure as a supervisor.

The first time Wayne turned in one of his assignments to me—a story I was writing that I'd asked him to fact-check—it was pretty bad. Wayne had clearly not paid attention to the Web site's style guide, and several of the things I'd asked him to look up were incomplete or not correct. Instead of handing it back to him and telling him which things to fix or update, I did it myself. I did this partly because I still believed doing something myself was the fastest way, and partly because I couldn't work up the nerve to walk up to Wayne holding a paper full of red marks and tell him that he'd done the assignment completely wrong. After a few weeks of this, Wayne got kind of cocky. He thought he must have been doing a great job because no one ever corrected him, told him he was wrong, or let him know when he was making mistakes. Worse than that, we were all inadvertently covering for him by fixing his errors ourselves instead of teaching him and helping him learn to do great work on his own.

A few months into Wayne's internship, an assistant position opened up at the company. Wayne got the job, in no small part because no one had ever complained about the quality of his work and the higher-ups figured that meant he was doing really well. I was happy for him, but I also realized his job was about to get a lot harder and that I had wasted several opportunities to teach him. Sure enough, once Wayne was responsible for turning in work to senior editors instead of assistants, they didn't waste any time pointing out mistakes in his work or telling him that he had done something wrong and needed to start over. Wayne was understandably hurt and frustrated—after all, he'd been doing the same level of work for months, with no one ever saying anything negative about it, and now all of a sudden people were telling him he was wrong?

The truth is, I was largely to blame for Wayne's struggles at work. I'd had many chances to tell him he was doing something wrong or explain company policy, but had never taken advantage of them. My fear of managing someone wasn't just my problem anymore—it had become his problem too. I could have nipped his problems in the bud, but because I couldn't or wouldn't allow myself to feel like a "boss" or "manager," Wayne's work suffered. And the first time a senior editor told him he was making significant errors and that his work was sloppy, Wayne was crushed. It was a huge blow for him because I'd let him spend several months thinking he was doing a great job. My refusal and inability to manage had hurt Wayne's career as much as it had hurt mine. The whole debacle—and FYI, he's now at the same company and doing pretty well—helped me learn some hard but important lessons about myself. I was going to have to learn how to manage people if I ever wanted to move up in my career, but I felt uncomfortable doing so.

One of the things I reiterate on STA is that bosses—as a subset of people—are not fundamentally bad. Plenty of them suck and treat you like dirt, but that's because of their personalities and not their job descriptions. However, one major cause of boss/assistant discord is the fact that

many bosses get promoted on the basis of their work or se-
niority or whatever and don't get any additional training in
management skills. Many bosses are still learning how to
do their jobs just as assistants are learning how to do *their*
jobs, and they're not at all ready to work with each other.
As one STA commenter put it, "From my experience,
promotion is treated like a video game at work. You are an
employee between 1–200 points. You start off at 1, and
depending on years of service, extra work, dedication,
smarts, and skills, you keep on adding points to your total.
Once you reach 201 points you're a manager!" While that's
not necessarily the case, this commenter made an excellent
point—lots of people get promoted into jobs they're not
capable of doing. Or, more likely, they're great at the job
and ready for the new responsibility but could probably use
some extra guidance or training for some of the new com-
ponents of their job—in particular, how to work with others and be a manager.

Since your job may give you a promotion into a leadership role regardless of how ready you are, here are a couple of things I learned from my disastrous initial attempt
at managing someone. Let's hope you do a better job than
I did.

Be honest. When your intern messes something up, let
him know. You can correct mistakes without yelling,
screaming, or being a jerk. If your intern is old enough

to have a proper job, then he is also old enough to handle a little criticism. Just make sure your comments are about his work performance, not about something personal.

You can also be honest about your own misgivings or apprehensions. You're totally allowed to say, "Sorry, I don't mean to be harsh about this, but I've never managed anyone before so I'm not great at explaining the procedure for how to do this. Do you have specific questions about what we're working on? Let's start with those."

Pretend she's a houseguest. Before you can start giving anybody work to do, make sure you've been a good host first. Pretend that the office is your house and the intern is a guest who's staying with you for a couple of days—what would she need/want to know? Make sure she knows where the bathroom is, how to log on to her e-mail, who she can talk to about an IT problem, how to work the coffee machine, and where she can hang up her coat. It may seem like really tedious stuff, but it all helps to make your intern feel welcome, comfortable, and like a true member of the company. Also, if she already knows the answers to basic questions, she'll be less likely to IM you when you're in the middle of something important to ask you what floor the cafeteria is on.

· · ·

Give him a heads-up on unwritten office rules and proto-col. Keep in mind that you've been at your job for a while, and so there are probably certain things about the company that you know but have never explicitly been told. Your intern is new to the company and may in fact be to-tally new to working in an office in general, so the least you can do is fill him in on what he should know but hasn't been told. Such unwritten rules can include things like the dress code ("I know it says in the employee hand-book that we're allowed to wear shorts in the summer, but the office manager will say something to you if they're too short . . . I actually had to go home and change once!"), how to act around the office's big cheeses ("The CEO never speaks to assistants or interns. He's just a douche, don't take it personally. If you need to ask him something just ask his assistant and she'll help you"), and who he can go to with problems or questions ("I know you're sup-posed to come straight to me, but if I'm in a meeting with my boss, he'll be pissed if you interrupt me. So feel free to go to Joey with questions in the meantime or wait for me and work on something else until I'm available").

It's okay to be friends. Odds are that you and your intern are closer in age than you and your boss. You and your intern might hit it off and end up becoming friends and hanging out outside of work—this is fine, as long as you're able to remain professional at the office. While you've successfully managed to be friends with some of your coworkers and not let it get in the way of your job performance, your intern probably doesn't have previous experience working in an office, and your own behavior and attitude will go a long way in helping her figure out what's appropriate.

Admit your own failings. Since I wasn't comfortable saying to an intern "Do this" or "Don't do that," I ended up softening the blow by combining the instruction with an anecdote or personal story. For example, instead of just saying, "Don't talk in meetings unless someone calls on you," which I thought sounded really harsh, I turned it into "You know, just an FYI, most of the assistants and interns don't really pitch in during meetings unless someone directly asks them a question. I mean, once I just butted in with an idea I had and it turned out my brilliant idea was the exact opposite of what the editor in chief wanted to do, and I was *so* embarrassed!" That way, you're not only giving the intern some advice about what to do, but assuring him that you were in his position once and can identify with how he feels. Plus, it will make you feel like you're offering constructive advice rather than being bossy or calling him out on something.

. . .

Make sure you know what the internship requirements are. If she's working for college credit, every school has its own system and rules about what is required. Check in with her and make sure everything's up to speed—do you need to sign some kind of paper verifying the number of hours she's worked? Does she need to work on only specific kinds of projects? Is there some kind of final paper or presentation she needs to complete in order to get her grade that someone at your company has to sign off on? Make sure you do your part to make sure that she is able to get full credit for her internship—she's helping you by taking on some of your work responsibilities, so the least you can do is help her get acknowledgment for the internship and proper credit for what she's doing.

Let interns feel like insiders. Yes, it's important for interns to learn how to do transcription and fill out contract request forms and do the boring and tedious stuff you don't have time for. But it's also important for interns to get a sense of what it's like to actually work at a company—and that includes more than just doing work. Inviting them along for happy hour (unless they're underage, of course), taking them out to lunch on their first day, or inviting them to the company holiday party is a great way to help interns feel included in *all* parts of the company. Besides, it's just plain mean to make people help you with all the planning and coordinating for an event and then not invite them.

Listen. When I look back on my experiences as an intern, I remember how much time I spent being utterly confused by even the simplest tasks. Stuff that everybody in the office could do in five minutes, like filling out an expense sheet, took me forever as I learned how to understand corporate jargon or struggled with multiple versions of the same document. When my internship coordinator came to check on me, I would end up asking her half a dozen questions about everything from punctuation to scheduling. Luckily, she was really understanding about my questions, and by the end of my internship I was a total pro who was put in charge of training the interns who came after me.

Even though something may seem easy to you now, you never know what questions, clarifications, or problems someone else is going to have. Before you walk over and start listing stuff that the intern needs to be working on, pause and see if he has any questions about existing assignments or even general stuff about the office. You'd be amazed by how much not knowing where staples are can derail a work in progress.

. . .

So, what have we learned? Whether you're an assistant for life, an aspiring executive, or something in between, there is a way. No matter how unhappy you are at your current gig or how much you think you're going to be trapped in a thankless job forever, this book is here to remind you that you possess the strength and ability to have the kind of career you want. It's not easy, but nothing extraordinary is ever easy. The tools in this book are yours to use, and I hope they help you figure out how to advance, retain your perspective, and make you laugh once in a while. Whether you're reminding yourself that it could be worse (perhaps it's time to use "At least I don't work for Naomi Campbell" as your mantra?), choosing a former-assistant-done-good role model whose career you want to emulate, or figuring out how to spot an Idea Thief before they swipe your brilliant proposal, this book will help you to navigate the assistant stage of your career. It's my hope that you won't need this book for long, but that the ideas here stay with you as you move up through the ranks and build a successful, rewarding career.

Above all, keep in mind the Rule of Assistant Karma—always treat assistants (and temps, and interns, and janitors, and receptionists, and everybody else who is "below" you on the office totem pole) as you wish you'd been treated when you were an assistant. The work you do now is laying the foundation for your career later on, and you don't want to destroy all that hard work by becoming a sucky boss. It may not seem like a lot, but changing one assistant's life for the better has a huge effect on your office. Imagine what would happen if bosses all over the world treated their assistants with courtesy and respect— let's just say this book wouldn't be necessary anymore, and I'd be pretty darn okay with that. Until then, put this book in your bag, get a good night's sleep, and go kick some ass on Monday morning.

Endnotes

5   *"Exhaled by culture"*: 2008 commencement address by Barbara Kingsolver. "How to Be Hopeful." 11 May, 2008. http://www.dukenews.duke.edu/2008/05/kingsolver.html

18   *Wintour had apparently insisted*: Gawker.com: "Anna Wintour Is Still a Hair Nazi." August 27, 2008. http://gawker.com/5042432/anna-wintour-is-still-a<->hair-nazi

27   *"Morale has been low"*: Park, Ed. *Personal Days: A Novel.* New York: Random House, 2008. Page 3.

74   *Of the thousands*: Jake Halpern, *Fame Junkies: The Hidden Truths Behind America's Favorite Addiction*: Houghton Mifflin, 2007, page 84.

76   *convicted of assault*: *New York Times*: "Naomi Pleads Guilty to Tossing Phone at Maid." January 17, 2007. http://www.nytimes.com/2007/01/17/nyregion/17naomi.html

76   *ordered to do community service*: BBC News: "Supermodel Naomi 'to mop floors.'" March 7, 2007. http://news.bbc.co.uk/2/hi/americas/6425581.stm

76   *expensive and inappropriate outfits*: MSNBC: "Campbell hangs up mop, straps on stilettos." March 23, 2007. http://www.msnbc.msn.com/id/17760892

76   *spotted in a shirt*: The Fashion Bomb: "Naomi Campbell Hit Me." March 2, 2009. http://fashionbombdaily.com/wp-content/uploads/2009/03/naomi_campbell_hit-me.jpg

77   *assistant had to clean up*: *New York Magazine*: "Talk Show Host Gives Birth." April 23, 2007. http://nymag.com/news/intelli gencer/30932/

78   *thinly veiled account*: *USA Today:* "'The Devil Wears Prada': Lauren Weisberger." April 15, 2005. http://www.usatoday.com/community/chat_03/2003-04-15-weisberger.htm

79   *attacked his other assistant*: TMZ: "Sex Pistol Accused of Firing Fist at Woman's Face." June 4, 2008. http://www.tmz.com/2008/06/04/sex-pistol-accused-of-firing-fist-at-womans-face/

79   *tried to physically attack*: The Huffington Post: "Artie Lange Walks Off Howard Stern, Possibly for Good." April 11, 2008. http://www.huffingtonpost.com/2008/04/11/artie-lange-walks-off-how_n_96187.html

79   *entered a rehab facility*: E! Online: "Artie Lange Enters Rehab." August 6, 2008. http://www.eonline.com/uberblog/b22427_artie_lange_enters_rehab.html

79   *carry around extra hot rollers*: The Insider: "Mariah Carey's Diet and Beauty Tips." September 24, 2007. http://www.theinsider.com/news/372625_Mariah_Carey_s_Diet_And_Beauty_Tips

79   *carry around breast tape*: Hollywood Rag: "Mariah Carey's Breast Tape Assistant." September 24, 2007. http://www.hollywoodrag.com/index.php?/weblog/mariah_careys_breast_tape_assistant/

80   *hold on to Mimi's drinking straw*: Contactmusic.com: "Mariah Carey Stuns Fans with Drinks Assistant." December 6, 2005. http://www.contactmusic.com/new/xmlfeed.nsf/story/carey-stuns-fans-with-drinks-assistant

80   *Twizzlers, raspberry seltzer, and nondairy creamer*: *New York Post*: "Seltzer Specific." June 20, 2008. http://www.nypost.com/p/pagesix/seltzer_specific_ySOTRJWILZtvXz2yvJtQKK

81   *hands over a card*: *New York Daily News*: "David Hasselhoff's

pickup game isn't that hot." April 16, 2008. http://www.nydaily
news.com/gossip/2008/04/16/2008-04-16_david_hasselhoffs_
pickup_game_isnt_so_ho.html

81   *very intoxicated and angry*: *People*: "Falling Apart." August 6,
2007. http://www.people.com/people/archive/article/0,,20061498,
00.html

81   *yelled at Jessica*: The Hollywood Gossip: "It's Lindsay Ratowsky:
Latest Lindsay Lohan Rival Revealed." December 8, 2006.
http://www.thehollywoodgossip.com/2006/12/its-lindsay-ra
towsky-latest-lindsay-lohan-rival-revealed/

82   *huge, star-studded baby shower*: *Mail* Online: "Detox Kate in tears
as she loses her 'rock.'" March 9, 2008. http://www.dailymail.co
.uk/tvshowbiz/article-528700/Detox-Kate-tears-loses-rock.html

82   *"trading places" for the day*: *Sun*: "Kate Mosses up her nanny's life."
August 7, 2008. http://www.thesun.co.uk/sol/homepage/show
biz/bizarre/article1524029.ece#OTC-RSS&ATTR=Bizarre

82   *wrote the introduction*: Davidbelisle.com: "Resume." Undated.
http://www.davidbelisle.com/resume

83   *such good friends*: News.com.au: "Kate Bosworth's wedded bliss
(sort of)." March 6, 2008. http://www.news.com.au/entertain
ment/story/0,26278,23327812-10388,00.html

83   *let her speak for herself*: Neilgaiman.com: "What My Assistant
Does." August 12, 2006. http://journal.neilgaiman.com/2006/
08/what-my-assistant-does.html

84   *he's a little person*: Mlive.com: "Chelsea Handler . . ." August 7,
2008. http://www.mlive.com/entertainment/flint/index.ssf/2008/
08/chelsea_lately_comedienne_take.html

84   *nabbed a book deal*: Goodreads: "Little Nuggets of Wisdom."
April 2009. http://www.goodreads.com/book/show/4412981
.Little_Nuggets_of_Wisdom

84   *That tune, "Terry's Song"*: Songfacts: "Terry's Song." Undated.
      http://www.songfacts.com/detail.php?id=9092

85   *happy and fulfilled*: Countingdown.com: "'*Sex and the City*' Cast
      and Director Interviews." March 19, 2008. http://www.count
      ingdown.com/features?feature_id=4032746

85   *a new car*: *New York Daily News*: "How to hit the road." July 18,
      2007. http://www.nydailynews.com/gossip/bwiddicombe/2007/
      07/18/2007-07-18_fanning_ushers_ire_.html

85   *The two got pregnant*: Bauer Griffin Online: "Angelina Jolie's Preg-
      nant Assistant, Same Due Date." March 23, 2008. http://bauerg
      riffinonline.com/2008/05/angelina-jolies-pregnant-assis.php

86   *Christian Bale and his wife*: Wikipedia: "Sandra (Sibi) Blazic."
      Undated. http://en.wikipedia.org/wiki/Sandra_Bla%C5%BEi%
      C4%87

86   *Elisha Cuthbert and her former fiancé*: IMDB: "Trace Ayala."
      Undated. http://www.imdb.com/name/nm1598767/

86   *former assistant to Sean Penn*: IMDB: "Alison Dickey." Undated.
      http://www.imdb.com/name/nm0225457/

86   *Alejandro Sanz and his reported wife*: Latin Gossip: "Did Alejan-
      dro Sanz Secretly Marry?" September 11, 2008. http://www
      .latingossip.com/alejandro-sanz/did-alejandro-sanz-secretly-
      marry.html

87   *When he retired*: *Miami Herald*: "Miami banker gives $60 million
      of his own to employees." February 14, 2009. http://www.miami
      herald.com/news/miami-dade/story/904842.html

87   *went one step further*: *Investment News*: "Singing an Assistant's
      Praises." March 24, 2008. http://www.investmentnews.com/
      apps/pbcs.dll/article?AID=/20080324/REG/538784977/1013

87   *redesigned his studio*: *Herald Sun*: "Molly Meldrum's got a little
      mate." March 29, 2008. http://www.heraldsun.com.au/news/

victoria/molly-meldrums-got-a<->little-mate/story-e6frf7kx-
1111115916946

88   *needed a kidney transplant*: "Boss Donates Kidney to Employee."
     June 20, 2007. http://abcnews.go.com/GMA/story?id=3297668&
     page=1

88   *top immediate priority*: *Variety*: "WMA Layoffs Begin." May
     18, 2009. http://www.variety.com/article/VR1118003877.html
     ?categoryId=13&cs=1

117 *Hime & Company*: Reuters: "Japanese firm offers 'heartache
     leave' for staff." January 28, 2008. http://www.reuters.com/arti
     cle/lifestyleMolt/idUST8913820080128

176 *allegedly bludgeoned her to death*: *New York Observer*: "The Stein
     Murder Confession." November 9, 2007. http://www.observer
     .com/2007/stein-murder-confession-marijuana-smoke-yoga-
     stick-kelloggs-diner

210 *feeling was mutual*: Writers Guild of America, West: "A Funny
     Thing Happened on the Way to Wisteria Lane." Undated.
     http://www.wga.org/writtenby/writtenbysub.aspx?id=1762

210 *writing a part for her*: IMDB: "Dixie Carter." Undated. http://
     www.imdb.com/name/nm0141581/

210 *Subversive Cross Stitch*: Save the Assistants: "The STA Interview:
     Julie Jackson." September 15, 2008. http://savetheassistants
     .com/2008/09/15/the-sta-interview-julie-jackson/

210 *Divabetic*: PR Newswire: "Novo Nordisk and Divabetic to In-
     spire Glamorous Diabetes Care." Undated. http://www.prnews
     wire.com/mnr/divabetic/31968/

211 *successful filmmaker in his own right*: IMDB: "Jonathan Levine."
     Undated. http://www.imdb.com/name/nm1349522/

211 *Rob Reiner's personal assistant*: Wikipedia: "Cheryl Hines." Un-
     dated. http://en.wikipedia.org/wiki/Cheryl_Hines

211 *Intern Queen*: Intern Queen Inc.: "About Me." Undated. http://www.internqueen.com/about.php

212 *no less than the Beatles*: *Los Angeles Times*: "Harvey Weinstein, 'Nowhere' Man." March 24, 2009. http://articles.latimes.com/2009/mar/24/entertainment/et-bigpicture24

212 *five years working as the assistant*: Karadioguardi.net: "Interesting facts about Kara DioGuardi." Undated. http://www.karadioguardi.net/kara-dioguardi-trivia.php

212 *SDT Waste and Debris*: National Public Radio: "In New Orleans, Trash Magnate Cleans Up." September 12, 2008. http://www.npr.org/templates/story/story.php?storyId=94567163

213 *Naughty Secretary Club*: Save the Assistants: "The STA Interview: Jen Perkins." May 18, 2009. http://savetheassistants.com/2009/05/18/the-sta-interview-jen-perkins/

213 *his first job*: Defamer: "Liveblogging the Oscars . . ." February 25, 2007. http://defamer.gawker.com/hollywood/oscars/liveblogging-the-oscars-here-we-go-again-239504.php

213 *became a tabloid presence*: IMDB: "Odessa Whitmire." Undated. http://www.imdb.com/name/nm0926208/

213 *Some Odd Rubies*: Someoddrubies.com: "Who We Are." Undated. http://someoddrubies.com/

214 *director Michael Moore*: IMDB: "Jason Pollock." Undated. http://www.imdb.com/name/nm1660671/

214 *his first documentary*: Theyoungestcandidate.com: "Director Jason Pollock to be honored . . ." July 28, 2009. http://www.theyoungestcandidate.com/main/News/tabid/58/EntryID/84/Default.aspx

214 *Jolie in NYC*: Wikipedia: "Nadine Haobsh." Undated. http://en.wikipedia.org/wiki/Nadine_Haobsh

214 *carrying P. Diddy's umbrella*: Contactmusic.com: "I'm An Assistant, Not a Butler." March 26, 2004. http://www.contactmusic .com/new/xmlfeed.nsf/story/p-diddy.s-bentley.-i.m-an-assistant-not-a-butler

214 *wrote a style book*: Amazon.com: "Advance Your Swagger." Undated.   http://www.amazon.com/Advance-Your-Swagger-Manners-Confidence/dp/1400064538/ref=sr_1_1?ie=UTF8&s=books&qid=1252291571&sr=8-1

214 *From G's to Gents*: MTV.com: "From G's to Gents." Undated. http://www.mtv.com/ontv/dyn/g_to_gents/series.jhtml

Erik Trinidad

LILIT MARCUS is the cofounder of SaveTheAssis tants.com and the editor of TheGloss.com. Her writing has also appeared in *Newsweek*, the *New York Post*, and on Mediabistro.com. She lives in New York City.